LIFETIME SPORT AND FITNESS SERIES

Self-Defense:
A Body-Mind Approach

Thomas Seabourne
Ernest Herndon

Gorsuch Scarisbrick, Publishers
Scottsdale, Arizona

Consulting Editor for the Lifetime Sport and Fitness Series: Robert P. Pangrazi, Chairman of the Department of Physical Education • Arizona State University

GV
1111
.S347
1987

Editor: *[...]chotanus*
Production Manager: *Gay Orr*
Manuscript Editor: *Barbara Farabaugh*
Cover Design: *Gordon Fong, The Omni Group*
Typesetting: *Carlisle Graphics*
Layout: *Bill Nebel, Graphic Arts Services*
Printing and Binding: *BookCrafters*

Gorsuch Scarisbrick, Publishers
8233 Via Paseo del Norte, Suite E-400
Scottsdale, Arizona 85258

10 9 8 7 6 5 4 3 2 1

ISBN 0-89787-603-2

Copyright © 1987 by Gorsuch Scarisbrick, Publishers

All rights reserved. No part of this publication may be reproduced, stored in a retrieval system, or transmitted, in any form or by any means, electronic, mechanical, photocopy, recording, or otherwise, without the prior written permission of the publisher.

Printed in the United States of America.

Preface

He who knows how to live can walk abroad
Without fear of rhinoceros or tiger.
He will not be wounded in battle.
For in him, rhinoceroses can find no place to thrust their horn,
Tigers no place to use their claws,
And weapons no place to pierce.
Why is this so?
Because he has no place for death to enter.

Lao-Tsu, *Tao Tê Ching*

Sun Lu-t'ang, a legendary Chinese martial arts master, once reportedly said, "One does not need strength to be a fighter." An elderly man at the time, Sun proved his point by easily thwarting a strong, energetic, young opponent.

Sun demonstrated that what was more important than strength were qualities such as technique, flexibility, balance, and inner stability. In *Self-Defense: A Body-Mind Approach,* we take a similar view. We encourage the development of physical strength, but we recognize that by the very nature of assault, a victim is likely to be weaker than the attacker.

Presented in this book are philosophies of self-defense; exercises designed to develop flexibility, balance, and strength; techniques for defending and attacking; an overview of recent scientific methods for achieving a state of relaxation during high stress; and cognitive strategies to prepare the student for crisis moments such as actual self-defense situations. All exercises and techniques are shown in clear, step-by-step form with detailed instructions and accompanying photographs.

Literally thousands of physical techniques are available to the dedicated practitioner of the martial arts. However, cognitive strategies, or mental techniques, are rarely dealt with in self-defense books or courses. As Sun Lu-t'ang demonstrated, however, mental preparation is an essential—indeed, perhaps the most essential—ingredient in self-defense. Our thirteen cognitive strategies provide the student with a variety of methods for learning to instill inner stability. As with physical techniques, mental techniques must be practiced and perfected so that they come readily when needed. For a physical technique to be effective when one is confronted by an attacker, it must come almost automatically, the result of much practice. The same is true of mental techniques that can avoid freeze-up or panic at a moment of attack.

By following the course outlined in this book, the dedicated student should acquire basic competence in self-defense skills. The confidence, alertness, and general freedom from fear that can result will overlap into other areas of life as well, and perhaps the gentle balance evinced by Sun Lu-t'ang will ultimately be achieved.

Using the Book

This book was written in order to provide students with a comprehensive guide to physical and mental self-defense strategies. The book contains a wide variety of physical techniques as well as numerous cognitive strategies to control stress and excitement levels.

There are several ways to use the book. The ideal would be to take a self-defense class using the book as a reference guide to accompany the direct training experience.

Another method would be to use the book step by step, practicing each skill until you have gained control before moving on to the next step. By this method you would proceed at your own pace through the entire book.

A third approach would be to examine the book, deciding which techniques may be most relevant to your specific needs. You could then orient your physical and mental skills training to those strategies.

In all cases, remember that practice is crucial in acquiring the physical skills. In addition, the mental strategies should be used in conjunction with the physical techniques so that both may become automatic in your self-defense repertoire.

Objectives

1. To improve physiological components including flexibility, muscular endurance, movement time, reaction time, power, balance, and coordination.
2. To instill psychological parameters including confidence, discipline, group dynamics, and self-control.
3. To learn physical strategies for active self-defense in street situations.
4. To become aware of passive resistance (noncombative) techniques for self-defense situations.
5. To introduce contemporary psychological strategies that may improve self-defense performance.

Acknowledgments

I would like to thank my parents, who let me begin my karate training by climbing over a barbed wire fence each evening to train with Zenpo Shimabuku in Okinawa. My training was further spurred by Soon Ho Chang, Vance McLaughlin, and Raymond McCallum, among others.

The "Cognitive Strategies" portion of this work had a tremendous contribution by Robert Weinberg, Ph.D., and David Yukelson, Ph.D.

All photographs herein were taken by Ernest Herndon except those in which he appears. Additional photographic assistance was provided by Danese Seabourne, Mike Williamson, Alexander Maillho, and Diana Tompkins. Thanks to Danese Seabourne, Angelyn Herndon, Andy Coy, and Diana Tompkins for appearing in these photographs.

Special thanks are due to Ernest Herndon's martial arts instructor, Cliff Ott.

Finally, I would like to thank Ernest Herndon for his gift for writing and the ability to transform technical jargon into readable information.

Tom Seabourne

Contents

PART ONE: Preparedness   1

1. Philosophy of Self-Defense: Armed and Dangerous   1
2. Street Awareness: Prevention, Preparedness, and Resistance   5

PART TWO: Techniques   11

3. Exercises   11
4. Basic Strikes   19
5. Blocks and Footwork   27
6. Combinations   35
7. Sparring   42
8. Grabs and Holds   47
9. Weapons   50
10. Home Practice   55

PART THREE: Cognitive Strategies   59

11. Ancient Wisdom   59
12. An Overview   61
13. The Jitters   63
14. Finding the Right Level   64
15. Relaxation and Imagery: VMBR   66

16 The Path to Relaxation   68
17 Concentration and "Flow"   71
18 Mental Techniques   73

PART FOUR: Evaluation Guide   80

Suggested Instructors' Evaluation Guide   80
Sample Rating Guide   80
Sample Tests   82

Appendix

Student Handouts: Individualized Self-Defense   84
Handout One: Performance
Handout Two: Performance
Handout Three: Sparring
Handout Four: Mental Techniques
Handout Five: Cognitive Strategy
Handout Six: Street Awareness

Bibliography   89

PART ONE
Preparedness

1
Philosophy of Self-Defense: Armed and Dangerous

The human body is a veritable arsenal of potent weapons. Until you learn what these weapons are and how they can be used, however, they must lie dormant. The time to learn about them is before they are most needed (i.e., in a crisis, which leaves little room for error).

Who has not seen the following scene on a television detective show: One man is choking another in a life-and-death struggle; the man being choked grips his assailant's strong arms in a gesture of futility, gasping as his life fades. It is safe to say that the person being choked is not in a position to start considering what "arsenal of weapons" his body might possess, especially considering that he may have only seconds of consciousness left.

However, had this victim received a modicum of training, he would have dispensed with struggling with his opponent's arms. Instead he might have jabbed directly to the hollow just below his attacker's Adam's apple, a technique that is devastating regardless of one's strength. Perhaps he would have tried any one of several other techniques, all of which are perfectly simple parts of the body's arsenal, but most of which are unknown to the untrained person.

We do not share the opinion of those who believe that a woman accosted by an assailant must necessarily go along with him passively. The reasoning behind such a view is that ineffective resistance will only anger the assailant, perhaps causing him to commit a crime worse than he had originally intended. Total submission is one aspect of the philosophy of passive resistance, a viable system that is discussed in detail in Chapter 2.

We agree, however, that unless a person knows what to do, he or she might do well to remain passive, just as a person who does not know how to use a gun would be ill-advised to try to use it during a moment of crisis. Shooting instructors know that one must be familiar with a gun before attempting to use it in a serious situation. When the time comes to use it, you must have no questions whatsoever in your mind about such details as whether the safety is on or off or how to put a shell into the chamber.

The same is true of the human body. A person familiar with self-defense techniques—many of them surprisingly simple—will be far better prepared to act when the need arises.

Of course, there are no guarantees: Self-defense experts have died at the hands of untrained assailants. A bullet from a .38-caliber handgun can out-do any technique, and a sharp knife can be very effective as well. However, a knowledge of self-defense techniques and of mental attitudes that must accompany them exponentially increases chances of survival.

What do we mean by mental attitude? Consider the very simple technique of the eye-jab. Few techniques are as effective as this. You simply stiffen your fingers and ram them into your assailant's eyes. It takes only a second. But if you think that by knowing how to perform the eye-jab move you are mentally equipped to perform this act on a living person, think again. One of us (Herndon) has survived an attempt by a street assailant to put out his eyes. Why? The assailant lacked the total commitment to carry through with the act; he merely went ineffectively through the motions.

An eye-jab, as with any technique, requires tremendous resolve. It hinges on a principle basic to martial arts: A practitioner strikes *through* his target, not *at* it. In breaking boards, the practitioner learns to aim several inches beyond the board, rather than at the surface of the board. Thus the board itself merely becomes something that is in the way, almost a superfluity. It is this principle that sometimes enables a trained child to break a board while a large, muscular man cannot. It is technique rather than brute force that succeeds.

This principle holds true with virtually any technique. Consider the palm-heel strike. If you strike *at* your opponent's nose with the palm-heel strike, you may flatten it against his face, causing pain and bleeding. Although it will hurt him, it quite possibly will not stop him. If, on the other hand, you aim at an imaginary target at the back of his head and drive your palm-heel *through* his nose—which has become in your mind a minor obstacle en route to your true target—you will smash his nose and drive his head violently back. The result will be far more effective.

Any technique requires utter resolve. You must be deeply committed to making the technique work; otherwise you may be programming it for failure. Are you capable of plunging your fingers into an attacker's eyes? That is a decision each individual must make. Can you actually kick through a person's knee? Are you capable of such violence? You will likely not know how you will feel until your safety, or that of loved ones, is actually threatened. If you know the technique and decide you cannot use it, then you have made your choice. However, if you do not know the technique, then you have no choice to make.

That is why we present these techniques. Techniques are alternatives. A master of self-defense may have a thousand alternative actions to any given situation, but only one or two may be required, and even a few well-practiced techniques that are thoroughly familiar to you will greatly increase your chances for survival in a life-and-death confrontation.

We said the body is an arsenal of weapons, but what are these weapons? (Perhaps you do not feel exactly like a walking munitions factory.) Well, the weapons are there, but they must be learned, and you must know how to unleash them. The unleashing involves the above-mentioned mental resolve. A technique, once unleashed, should be as unerring as a bullet fired from a gun.

Consider some of these weapons, all of which are presented more thoroughly in this text. You have elbows. Bend an arm and feel the elbow. It is unyielding. It is as hard as an oak cudgel, and it comes to a point that is capable of devastating penetration. Imagine the effect that elbow would have on someone's respiratory processes if it were slammed upward into an assailant's solar plexus, powered by all the strength of your legs, hips, shoulders, and back. Imagine it swinging around in an arc straight into someone's temple. The elbow is a formidable weapon that is capable of instantly disabling someone.

The fist is a weapon. The palm-heel, the fingers, thumbs, knees, and feet are all weapons. The crest of the head where the hairline meets the forehead is a hard bludgeon that can be used with painful effect on the much softer area of an attacker's face.

However, weapons are useless if they are not aimed at the proper target. The bullet from a .38-caliber pistol is deadly—unless it misses. If you shoot an assailant in the fleshy part of his side, you may well have an angry assailant on your hands, but if you shoot him in the heart or forehead he will pose no further threat.

The same is true of other self-defense techniques. You may have a fast, powerful front kick, but if you land it on the rock-hard midsection of a well-developed man, you will have severely compromised yourself. If, on the other hand, you direct that kick into his groin or against his knee, breaking the joint, you will have used your weapon effectively.

Just as the body contains weapons, it also contains targets, and these must be learned just as techniques must be learned. You should not head-butt someone's breastbone, jab his arm, or punch his shoulder. When you unleash your technique, it must be aimed precisely and unerringly toward a target that is exposed and that will be most vulnerable to its effects. If a man stands with his fists curled in front of his chest, it is futile to kick at the solar plexus. Look for the open spot. If he keeps his hands up in front of his face, why try an eye-jab?

The logic of these concepts can be grasped with ease, but to learn these techniques fully, you must practice them—the body must learn along with the mind. The body must be able to deliver a technique of its own accord. In a situation involving intense fear and danger, you are not likely to be able to think clearly and dispassionately, calmly picking out vulnerable target areas and choosing the technique that will work best. Response or attack must come automatically, and this can be learned only through practice.

It is for this reason that a partner is important during many parts of self-defense training. It is one thing to practice a kick in the air, but do you know what it is actually like to land a kick on someone?

Training aids such as kicking bags are also important. A kick practiced on another person will aid timing and aim, but when you kick a bag you can use all your strength. You must experience how it feels to land a hard, powerful technique.

What about the situation in which you are confronted with someone holding a gun or knife? Is not passive submission advisable then?

Passive submission is just one technique among many. It may well be necessary to use that technique for a time, but if the occasion arises when that technique is no longer feasible, you should use another. Watch and wait. Your mind must focus on the purpose of survival. Physically attacking your opponent is one alternative. Passive submission is another. Running away may be a viable alternative. In short, you must do what seems most likely to succeed at the time. Because the circumstances surrounding an assault are constantly changing, you must always be ready to change tactics.

If you climb into your car, start the engine, and suddenly feel a knife at the nape of your neck, that is not the time to try an eye-jab. Passive submission seems to be the technique called for at that moment. However, when the car is stopped and you are required to get out, the opportunity may arise for a physical technique.

Your body contains weapons, but they are not all attacking weapons. A scream may be a viable technique. As with any other, it must be performed with total commitment. A scream can be emitted that is so startling and loud that it can mentally disarm an opponent, not to mention alert people for blocks.

Your two feet, for running, are excellent "weapons." Your psychological cunning, the words you use, and the way you behave—anything that will aid you to survive, from passive submission to a lightning-fast eye-jab, from a scream to a knee in the groin—all are viable techniques of self-defense, and none should be neglected.

The body alone does not comprise all the weapons available to you. Many seemingly insignificant objects can enhance the body's effectiveness. The sharp spike of a high-heeled shoe can render a front kick many times more effective. A pencil or keys rammed into the eyes are even more unyielding than stiffened fingers. Slamming a purse at an opponent's head may be an excellent feint to draw his guard up and allow you to strike to the knee or groin. A chair, a broomstick, a piece of drainpipe, and even the diamond on an engagement ring may prove to be usable weapons.

This, then, is our goal: to introduce you to ways of thinking and acting so that in a life-threatening situation you will realize that you are, in fact, armed and dangerous.

2
Street Awareness: Prevention, Preparedness, and Resistance

One woman told us that she resents having to worry about rape. She said that she felt it was a sad state of affairs that a woman in this age, living in purportedly one of the world's most civilized nations, has to be on guard when going to the corner grocery for a box of ice cream. This woman was not inexperienced with assault. She had been attacked by an armed assailant, whom she fortunately had managed to elude without violence, because he had been chased off by her boyfriend. Such an incident would certainly leave emotional scars, and it probably heightened this woman's awareness of the dangers of modern life.

We agree with her in principle. It is sad that persons cannot feel free to pursue their everyday activities without a lurking fear of attack by some unknown assailant. However, we must face facts as they are. The danger of rape, assault, or other violence, although statistically slim, is there for everyone. As with a disease like cancer, it seemingly can strike anyone at any time with no rhyme or reason.

However, there are ways of lessening the chances for such attacks: simple shifts in habit coupled with a basic understanding of assault. According to information presented by the Houston Police Department, the vast majority of rapists are "power rapists." A smaller percentage are "anger rapists," and the remaining few are "sadistic rapists." These sadistic rapists—those who murder and perform other atrocities on their victims—receive the majority of the attention. Before we address the changes in habit that can reduce the chances of victimization, let's examine these types of rapists.

The power rapist, like virtually all rapists, does not have sexual desire as his primary motivation. The consensus among most authorities is that the significant motivating factor in rape is not sexual. Rape springs from anger and a desire to dominate.

Power rapists get their thrill from having power over their victims. They are planners, relying on schedules. In fact, it is this common factor that usually leads to their demise. For example, a power rapist whose strategy is climbing through the window of a house and raping the female inhabitant will most likely use that strategy all the time, giving authorities something to anticipate.

From the potential victim's viewpoint, this need for a preplanned schedule can be used against the rapist. To begin with, women should consider varying their own routines. Take different routes to work and other places. Be creative; don't fall into ruts of established behavior.

Anger rapists express hostility and contempt and enjoy degrading and injuring their victims. This anger is unrelated to the victim's behavior. Sadistic rapists are bent unvaryingly on violence, murder, and/or mutilation.

Statistically, a woman victimized by a rapist most likely is confronting a power rapist, who is not necessarily intent on doing injury other than the rape itself.

As mentioned, there are many ways to prevent rape, or to lessen chances of its happening. Here are a number of tips:

- Don't put yourself into needlessly vulnerable situations. Have your keys ready when approaching your vehicle. Use customer pickup services at stores if feasible.
- Install bars on windows at home and use effective locks on doors. More than half of rapes are estimated to occur in the home.
- Do not answer a knock on the door without being certain of who is there. If the person refuses to identify himself through the locked door, call the police.
- When out, make use of automatic systems that will cause your house lights to go on and off at specified times.
- If you live alone, list yourself by initials rather than first name in the telephone directory and on the mailbox.
- Do not pick up hitchhikers or stop to help someone with car trouble; proceed to an open place of business and report the breakdown from there.
- Keep car doors locked. Check the back seat before entering your vehicle.
- If your vehicle breaks down, raise the hood and stay in your vehicle with the doors locked and the windows up. When someone stops, roll the window down just enough to talk and ask the person to phone a relative, friend, garage, or police station.
- If you are being followed in a vehicle, drive to the nearest open place of business for help. Honk the horn and call attention to yourself. Pay attention to license numbers.
- Do not allow strangers into your home. Keep all entrances well lighted. Be aware that many rapes are committed by people acquainted with the victim.
- Avoid walking alone. Walk with someone or in areas where others are near.
- Do not walk alone if you are upset, drunk, or high on drugs.
- Avoid walking through deserted places.
- Hang up immediately on obscene phone callers.
- Park in well-lighted areas.
- When walking or traveling, remain alert. Do not put yourself in compromising circumstances. Be constantly aware of escape routes and places of potential ambush.
- Walk with a confident, assertive air. There is no question but that humans and animals are capable of exuding a sense of victimization. In the animal kingdom, creatures sense fear; the same holds for humans. Even if you feel fear, attempt to remain outwardly calm.

Tips such as those above often prompt a variety of objections. First, they seem to imply that we live in a sort of war zone, always prone to attack. We suggest a slightly different way of looking at things. All creatures practice similar techniques as a rudimentary part of survival. Even a housecat, if you will notice, remains alert and aware of what goes on around it. We suggest heightened awareness, not intensified fear. The dominant feeling should not be a creeping fear that one is about to be attacked, but instead a vivacious alertness characteristic of all healthy, intelligent creatures. Be aware that in fact you are not a helpless potential victim. Instead, know that you are capable of dealing with danger if it arises. Do not go about shrinking with terror, but look around and be aware of the world around you—its beauties as well as its dangers.

Second, some object that such tips are too involved to remember, much less put into practice. We submit that it is as easy to learn to look into the back seat of your car as it is to learn not to look there, and the possible consequences of negligence should not be ignored. Such behavior as listed consists in alternatives to already established habits. Instead of trying to follow these tips one by one, in a rote fashion, we suggest first a shift in attitude that predisposes you to a heightened awareness; these changes will then come easily.

A third reaction to such tips is a carefree shrug and an attitude that the chances of rape are slim, so why bother? This is generally a view held by women who have never been accosted or threatened. We suggest that the preferred time to become aware of the dangers of assault is before, not after, an assault occurs.

Now, suppose you find yourself confronted by an apparent rapist, despite any precautions you might have taken. A wide variety of alternatives exists, and which one is chosen depends on a number of factors. What type of rapist does he appear to be? Is he armed? If so, does he seem intent on using his weapon? How prepared are you to resist him physically? Would the dangers outweigh the hope of escape? Are you willing to submit to rape in hopes of avoiding even greater physical danger? Or do you fear that, in this situation, submitting to rape might also entail greater violence?

What about your surroundings? Is there anyone nearby, within shouting distance? Are there any potential weapons you might use?

What about the rapist's apparent state of mind? And your own? What appears to be at stake?

Basically, as mentioned in Chapter 1, there are two philosophies of response to assault: passive resistance and active resistance. There is more to passive resistance than blind submission. Many psychological factors may come into play. For instance, one woman threw her assailant into a state of disorientation by dropping to all fours and barking like a dog. This is based on a simple hypnotic procedure, which entails putting a subject into a hypnotic trance by performing a totally unexpected act. The late patriarch of hypnosis, Milton Erikson, once reportedly tried this principle when he rounded a street corner at 7:15 in the morning and bumped head-on into another pedestrian. Ever alert and ready to try new techniques, Erikson promptly looked at his watch and said, "It's 2:30." Then he walked briskly by. When he turned and looked, he saw the man standing there bewildered, speechless, and momentarily incapacitated—in other words, hypnotized.

Other techniques in the repertoire of passive resistance include vomiting or urinating on yourself to make yourself repugnant; telling the rapist you have venereal disease or cancer; telling him you're pregnant; feigning symptoms of serious illness such as heart attack (this must be realistic and convincing, however); feigning utter hysteria; pretending to go along with him and asking to go get a drink or a contraceptive device, and then leaving; or even trying some unexpected statement like, "Please don't rape me. My father raped me when I was a child."

Such techniques require an awareness and an ability to commit oneself totally, comparable to the commitment required for physical resistance. Other techniques include screaming, running away, and trying to talk the rapist out of his intentions.

Active resistance entails physical attack on your assailant. Just as with psychological techniques, it is best if you are familiar with these physical techniques ahead of time. When you commit yourself to attack, the following principles are necessary: keep your own vital areas protected; attack a vital, open spot on your assailant; get his weapon out of the way if he is armed; and follow up with a volley of techniques.

Use weapons available to you, be they fingernails or tire tools. It may be worse than useless to flail at an opponent without rhyme or reason, especially considering that a male attacker is likely to be bigger and stronger, not to mention more experienced in fighting, than his victim. Use techniques you know will work, like a jab into the eyes. Do not rely on a single technique. Follow up immediately with something else. Suppose your eye-jab misses. A knee to the groin delivered in the next instant will remedy that problem. Then follow with a stomp to the instep, a kick to the knee, and flight.

Detailed techniques for physical resistance are discussed in part 2.

Besides the conscious techniques of prevention and resistance, there are other, more subtle ways of preparation involving the subconscious mind. These are discussed in part 3, but basically they involve preparing the subconscious mind, through step-by-step, easily followed techniques, to guide you through situations in which your conscious mind may be paralyzed with fear. What is the good of knowing how to perform a front kick if your mind and body are so paralyzed with terror that you cannot even remember your own name?

Although your conscious mind may break down, however, your subconscious can be trained to take over for you, just as it frequently does in emergencies. By inducing states of relaxation, you can guide yourself or be guided into imaginary situations in which you will respond effectively to an assailant. Your subconscious mind will establish a program of action so that, regardless of the paralysis you may feel in a dangerous situation, you will be capable of adequate response.

Let's take a look at an imaginary situation of an ordinary woman confronted by a potential rapist and examine it step by step, keeping in mind the principles discussed so far.

> Joan has had a hard day at work, and now she needs to stop at the grocery store on her way home to pick up a few items for supper. It is dusk when she pulls her car into the vast parking lot of a supermarket. She locks her car, goes in, and returns with a sack of groceries in each arm. By now it is nearly dark. At her car, she sets one bag on the hood while getting her keys out. Before she can insert her car key into the lock, she feels a cold touch at the back of her neck. Turning around with a start, she sees a young man facing her, a knife in one hand. "Hey, baby," he says with a grin, "Let's you and me take a walk."
>
> Too paralyzed with fear to think of resistance or escape, Joan allows herself to be led by the elbow across the dark parking lot and behind the large building. Other than a few

bins of garbage, a locked service door, and a drainage ditch, there is nothing but darkness behind the brick, windowless store building.

We'll take a break here to examine the situation thus far. Could Joan have forestalled this situation, and if so, how?

To begin with, she could have had her keys ready to enter the car promptly, lessening the time available for the man to reach her from his unknown hiding place. Had she been more alert, she might have spotted the man before he had time to menace her. Also, she might have had an attendant carry her bags out for her.

Once confronted, had she had the presence of mind, she could have reacted in a number of ways. A violent scream, coupled with hurling her bag of groceries into the man's face and a mad dash across the parking lot probably would have ended the situation. It would be unlikely for the man to chase a screaming woman toward a well-lighted store full of people. However, such initiative was not forthcoming, because the woman felt paralyzed with fear and entertained the hope that some other means of escape would present itself later.

During the walk across the parking lot, she had other potential means of escape. As the man walked beside her, gripping her left arm with his right hand and holding his knife in his left hand, the woman might have considered a number of physical options, including breaking his hold by applying a sudden jerk with her arm against the weak part of his grip, the thumb, followed either by instant flight and screams, or by a more risky jab to the eyes, stomp to the knee, and takedown.

However, the woman, too frightened to act, allowed herself to be led beyond the relative safety of the parking lot and into the dark, deserted area behind the store.

Once there, she found herself face to face with a man, armed with a knife, who was evidently intent on not wasting time. She still had time to act, although such action would have been dangerous because it was dark and he faced her with a knife in hand. Nevertheless, a swift and decisive jab with stiffened fingers into his eyes, or perhaps a powerful palm-heel strike to his face, would have negated his ability to strike, especially if she followed with a knee to the groin and then grasped his head securely and wrenched it and then ran.

But Joan, although she had had minimal training in such techniques, heretofore had not felt prepared to use them. Now, confronted by imminent rape, she is still undecided about the danger posed by her assailant and wonders if rape alone will satisfy him.

In the darkness behind the building, the man grips his knife firmly and orders Joan to undress. She feels that, at the moment, the time for physical resistance has passed, because none of her training has prepared her to attack a man holding a knife a few inches away. Nevertheless, her mind spins into gear, and she begins to talk compulsively as she takes off her jacket. She tries to talk the man into letting her go, telling him it's a foolish risk, that he'll wind up in jail, and so forth. He does not respond, but merely watches her.

As Joan holds her jacket in her hand, she instinctively feels that if she does not act now, she will surely be raped and possibly stabbed. Realizing that her best defense is the jacket in her hand, she grips it tightly and wraps it around the man's knife hand, negating for a moment the danger of that weapon. Without pausing, she thrusts her leg violently upward between his legs, and then slams the crest of her head forward into his face. She pushes him back with her hands, and while he is temporarily off guard and injured, she flees into the parking lot, screaming.

Joan, albeit a little belatedly, has acted to save herself, and she has fortunately gotten away with it. It would have been possible for the man to have resisted her attack effectively and leave her dying behind the store. However, having weighed the risks in the situation, Joan had decided it was better for her to attack then and risk being killed than to surrender passively to rape and possible murder. Had the man been unarmed, or had she been convinced he meant no violent injury, she might have submitted to the rape, preferring to contend with the emotional trauma that rape can engender. She had felt that passive resistance and talking were getting her nowhere, and she was afraid to risk any verbal technique bordering on the bizarre.

Although she had felt that her final moment for action had arrived when she had removed her jacket, in fact there could have been several more opportunities for resistance. Even if she had been prone beneath her assailant, she could have tried eye-jabs, knees to the groin, head butts, and head wrenching. Had he held her arms pinned, with his weight on her torso, she might have moved her arms suddenly, shifting his weight, and thrown him off with her hips, following up with a strike to the groin and flight. Had he held her arms pinned with his weight at her groin, she might have thrust her arms out, causing him to lose his balance, and followed with a hard head butt to the face. However, it appears that in this situation the more time that elapsed the more risky active resistance became, and on reflection it appears that the best time for resistance, either active or passive, was in the parking lot.

PART TWO
Techniques

3
Exercises

A flexible body is essential in a self-defense situation. The following exercises should be practiced in order to make your body as flexible as your potential will allow. Keep these guidelines in mind as you follow a flexibility regime:

- Use static stretching techniques rather than ballistic movements. In other words, do not bounce as you attempt to stretch; instead, slide ever so slowly into position.
- Attempt to remain as relaxed as possible throughout your stretching routine.
- Keep your lower back from bending when you stretch, bending at the hips instead.
- Stretch to the point of tension, not pain.
- Warm up by stretching before a rigorous workout.
- Following a rigorous workout, stretching can be extremely beneficial because muscles will be warm.

Here are a number of valuable exercises:

1. Side Leg Stretch: (Purpose—to warm up the muscles of the inner thigh.) Keep the supporting foot flat and let yourself stretch to your limit. Do not stretch to the point of pain; instead go only until you reach a point of tension. As you get better at this exercise your stretch will go increasingly deeper.

1

2. Side Split: (Purpose—to improve flexibility in the groin muscles and facilitate kicking ability.) Focus your concentration on the inner thigh muscles; let them relax. Begin by spreading your legs as far as possible, letting your body weight and gravity force you lower until you reach a point of tension. Move slowly without jerking and hold at the point of tension for thirty seconds.

3. Front Split: (Purpose—to improve flexibility of the hamstring and improve performance for kicking techniques.) Perform the side stretch and then simply turn the toes up, putting tension on the hamstrings. Keep the feet spread as far apart as possible and hold this position for thirty seconds.

2

3

4. Front Split, chest to floor: (Purpose—to enhance further flexibility of the hamstring and groin in order to improve kicking strategies.) While performing the front split, slowly begin to drop the chest forward toward the floor. Be sure to keep your back as straight as possible. When you reach the point of tension, hold for thirty seconds.

5. Front Split, forehead to shin: (Purpose—to increase flexibility of the hamstring and groin, causing an increase in kicking ability.) From the front split position, use your right arm to pull across your body so that your chest will be drawn toward your left knee and your forehead toward your left shin. Attempt to keep your back straight without any sudden or bouncing movements. Go only until you reach the point of tension and hold for fifteen seconds. Repeat with the other side.

4

5

6. Butterfly: (Purpose—to warm up the groin muscles before practicing intense stretching exercises.) Sitting with the back straight and feet together as close to your groin as possible, grab your toes and slowly let your knees fall downward toward the floor.

7. Forehead to Toes: (Purpose—to stretch the lower back and hip muscles in order to prepare for vigorous physical activity.) From the butterfly position, grab your toes and begin to pull your forehead toward the floor in front of you. Attempt to keep your back straight as your chest leads in pressing toward the floor. Remember to breathe naturally from the diaphragm, exhaling on the way down.

6

7

8. Knees to Ground: (Purpose—to stretch the hips and groin area.) Again from the butterfly position, grab your toes and place your elbows on the inside of your knees. Press slowly and equally on your knees with your elbows. Continue until you reach the point of tension, and then hold for thirty seconds.

9–12. Pushups, fingertip and knuckle: (Purpose—to increase muscular strength and endurance in the triceps, wrists, and pectoral muscles, to increase gripping ability, and to toughen the knuckles for punching.) Lying on your stomach, spread your feet a little more than shoulder width. Extend your fingertips onto the floor in front. Attempt to keep your back straight as your elbows bend to let you perform each pushup. Work up to at least ten repetitions. Repeat, bearing the weight on the first two knuckles of each hand rather than the fingertips. Be sure to keep fingertips rigid on fingertip pushups and to let only the first two

8

9

10

11

12

knuckles of each hand touch the floor on knuckle pushups. Remember to go through the full range of motion, flexing and extending as your triceps and pectoral muscles expand and contract. Exhale as you push up, and inhale as you relax on the way down.

13, 14. Lateral Abdominal: (Purpose—to improve muscular endurance of the abdominal area to enable you to cock your leg most efficiently as well as to improve your confidence to take a strike.) Sitting with your knees bent and your feet secured, interlock your fingers behind your head. With your back straight, lean back midway to the floor and hold the position until intense tension is reached. Next, holding your fists in front of you, twist from side to side, working the abdominal muscles.

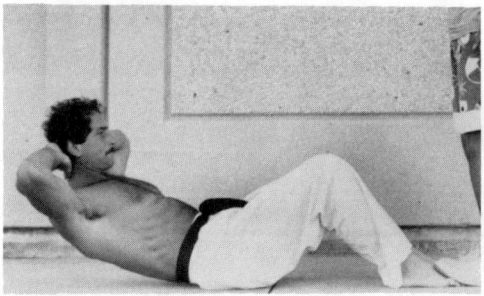

13

14

15, 16. V-Situps: (Purpose—to strengthen the medial abdominal muscles as well as the hip flexors.) Sit with the knees bent and your back at a 45-degree angle. Extend your legs about six inches above the floor until your knees are straight. Make sure to keep your back straight and concentrate on flexing the abdominal muscles as you extend your legs. Remember always to keep your feet at least six inches off the ground. Perform ten to twenty repetitions.

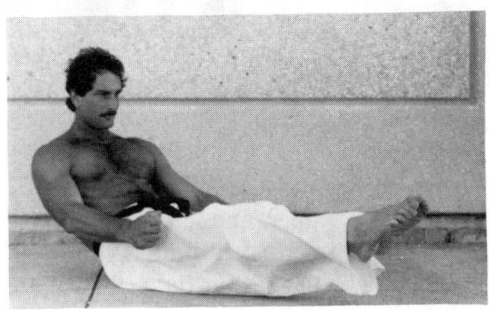
15

16

17. Flutter Kicks: (Purpose—to improve lower abdominal strength and hip flexor lifting capabilities.) Lie flat on your back and then raise your head and shoulders off the ground. Put your hands on your stomach and force your lower back to remain flat on the floor. Begin by raising your right leg, keeping the knees straight, from the ground to ten inches above the ground. Next lower your right leg until it is about two inches from the ground while you raise your left leg to ten inches. Continue this exercise as your legs flutter up and down in a reciprocal motion, never letting your feet touch the floor.

18-20. Lateral Leg Swings: (Purpose—to strengthen the lateral abdominal muscles as well as to improve your ability to cock each leg.) Lie flat on your back with your arms directly out to your sides. Raise your head and shoulders off the ground, keeping your lower back flat on the floor. Next raise your feet up to 90 degrees, keeping your knees straight. With your feet together, swing your legs over to the right, keeping your legs together, until they are two inches from the ground. At this point immediately swing the legs back over toward the left side until they are two inches above the ground. Continue exercising until the lateral abdominals have reached muscular failure.

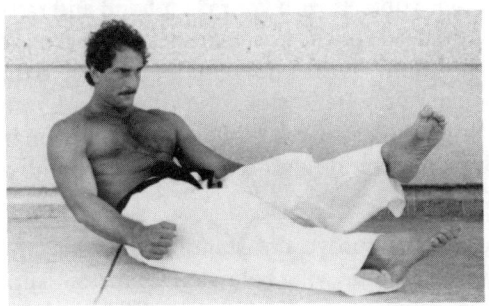
17

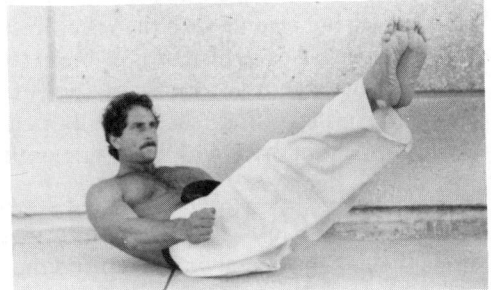
18

19

20

21. Cross Crunch: (Purpose—to improve lower, medial, upper, and lateral abdominal muscular endurance.) Lie flat on your back with your fingers interlocked behind your head and your knees bent in the air. Keep your lower back flat as you move your right elbow up to your left knee. Do not lower the back as you move your left elbow to your right knee. Remember to maintain constant tension in the abdomen as you continue this exercise in a reciprocal motion. Continue exercising until your frontal and lateral abdominals reach muscular failure.

21

22, 23. Roundhouse Kick with support: (Purpose—to improve roundhouse kicking ability by strengthening the hip muscle and lateral quadricep muscle as well as improving balance.) Use a chair or the wall for stability as you brace yourself with your right hand and raise your left leg up, leading with the knee. Keep the lateral side of the knee parallel to the ground with the knee raised as high as possible in the fold position. As the knee remains parallel to the ground, extend your left foot, striking your imaginary opponent with either the ball of your foot or the instep. After reaching full extension, bring the foot back to the cocked position in the fold. Continue this with each side until the hip and lateral thigh reach muscular failure. Repeat with right leg.

24, 25. Side Kick with support: (Purpose—to improve the standing side kick by strengthening the lateral quadricep and the hip as well as improving balance.) Grab your support with your right hand as you raise your left knee as high as you possibly can. With the knee raised, extend the left foot directly to the side, striking an imaginary opponent with the heel of the foot. After the leg reaches full extension, with the foot parallel to the ground, immediately bring it back to the high knee-fold position. Continue extending and flexing the leg until your hip and lateral thigh reach muscular failure. Repeat with other side.

22 23

24 25

26. Rotating Knees: (Purpose—to loosen up the lower quadricep and collateral ligaments of the knees prior to training.) Standing with your feet together and knees slightly bent, put your hands on the tops of your knees. Flex your knees about three inches to the front and let your knees rotate to the right. Continue turning the knees for a total of ten repetitions. Repeat with the same procedure going to the left.

27. Trunk Twister: (Purpose—to warm up the waist and hip area prior to physical training.) Stand with your feet shoulder-width apart. Extend your arms directly to the front, with the palms of the hands facing one another. Rotate laterally from the trunk while keeping the toes pointing straight ahead. Rotate first to your right side and then to your left. Continue for ten rotations to each side.

26

27

28

28. Windmill: (Purpose—to warm up the shoulder girdle in preparation for physical activity.) Standing with your feet pointing straight ahead and your knees slightly bent, extend your right arm over your head as your left arm brushes your left side. Keep your arms straight as you rotate them from the shoulder in a circular motion forward. Repeat this sequence for ten repetitions, then perform in the opposite direction for ten repetitions.

29. Squats: (Purpose—to strengthen the quadriceps and stretch the Achilles tendon.) With your feet shoulder-width or less apart, put your hands on your hips. Extend your arms to the front as you keep your feet flat and bend your knees to a 90-degree angle. Come back up to a standing position, bringing your arms back so that your hands are on your hips. Perform ten repetitions.

Note: Remember to exhale at the climax of each stretch. If abnormally sharp pains develop, seek the advice of a physician.

29

4
Basic Strikes

Hands, feet, elbows, knees—the correct use of these and other body parts can turn the human body into a formidable weapon. In striking an opponent or assailant, it is important to keep these principles in mind:

- Hit fast and hard to the target area (for example, the opponent's knee, groin, throat, eyes, solar plexus, nose, etc.).
- Maintain an attitude of relaxed concentration as you deliver the strike. Keep muscles relaxed until the moment of impact, when they should become tense and rigid. Relaxed muscles allow for faster movement and less energy consumption.
- As you strike, attempt to protect your body with your remaining extremities. For example, as you strike with a front kick, be prepared to block with your arms.
- Assume a properly balanced position immediately before striking with punches or kicks.
- Use as much deceptiveness as possible as you deliver your strikes so that your opponent will not see them until it is too late.
- Snap your strikes to the target area and then immediately retract them in case you must follow up with another technique.
- When practicing your strikes, imagine an opponent in front of you, and see yourself "exploding" your technique to the target.
- Always have a target for your strikes.

Here is a look at some basic striking techniques:

1. Palm-Heel Strike: The palm-heel strike should be aimed at the soft part of the nose in an attempt to drive the nasal bone up at a 45-degree angle. This is a good, hard, bludgeoning strike requiring little physical strength to be successful. It is especially good for women or those with weak wrists because the wrist cannot give (as with a punch). Add power to the strike by using your hips. Turn your hips with the strike, as though power surges from your rear foot up through the body, channeled out through the striking hand.

1

2. Hook Punch: The hook punch is a fast and deceptive technique. Because it comes in from an angle, it is difficult to block. It should be delivered with the front or lead hand. From the sparring position, pivot on the ball of the front foot so that the feet are parallel. Strike with the first two knuckles.

2

3. Jab: The jab is another fast technique delivered with the front hand. It is particularly useful for setting up the opponent for another, more powerful, technique such as the front kick or reverse punch. From the sparring position, go straight to the target and snap the fist back as quickly as it is delivered. Strike with the first two knuckles for penetration.

3

4. Elbow Strike: The elbow strike is an extremely powerful technique, to be used when you are too close to punch or kick. The elbow must be thrown with the body, so that your body weight is behind the strike. If possible, use your other hand as reinforcement, enabling you to strike with a perfect power chain. The elbow strike can be delivered from a wide variety of angles: across into the face; back to the temple; straight up into the solar plexus; down to the face, throat, or collarbone; or directly behind you into the solar plexus or groin.

4

5. Spinning Backfist: This is a fast, explosive, and deceptive technique. From a sparring position, twist the body suddenly and use your arm as a whip with your fist as the striking force. Make sure you see your target before you strike. Strike with the first two knuckles.

5

6. Knife-Hand Strike: From the sparring position, lift your hand up to your ear as if you were throwing a baseball. Shoot the open hand straight toward the target, twisting the hand just before contact. Strike with the meaty portion of the side of the hand between the wrist and the joint of the little finger. Strike horizontally to the neck or vertically to the collarbone.

6

7. Eye-Jab: This is a simple and devastating technique, but it requires explosive speed and utter commitment to be successful. From the sparring stance, make your middle finger and index finger as rigid as possible, keeping them slightly bent at the joints. Strike straight and fast directly at the eyes with a quick, relaxed motion. When contact with the eyes has been made, dig deep into the sockets and grab the face for control. Variants of the eye-jab include stiffening all four fingers and striking at the bridge of the opponent's nose so that the fingers separate, with two plunging into each eye, and bending the fingers at the middle knuckles in order to claw in the manner of an eagle's talons.

7

8. Reverse Punch: From the sparring position, use the rear hand as the punching force. Let the hips twist, initiating the action, and let the power flow through your body and explode

8

through the striking hand. Stay as relaxed as possible until the moment of impact. Use the first two knuckles for penetration and a twist of the wrist for torque. This is a powerful technique and can be used with good effect against the body of an attacker.

9. Side Kick Fold: From the sparring position, raise the knee to a cocked position without bending at the waist. Do this as quickly and deceptively as possible without telegraphing your shift in body weight. With the knee in this position, your body is protected from attack.

10. Side Kick: From the cocked position, extend the foot straight to the target. Twist the hip for added power. Hit fast and hard, striking with the heel of the foot. This powerful kick can be used against an attacker's leg to shatter his knee. It is also a good defensive strike to groin, solar plexus, or ribs.

9 10

11. Front Kick Fold: From a sparring position, raise the foot up to knee level as quickly as possible without bending at the waist. With the knee in this position, your body is protected from attack.

11

12. Front Kick: Extend the foot straight to the target, maintaining the arms in a position that will protect your body. Bring the foot back as quickly as the kick is delivered in order to protect yourself against a counterattack. Strike with the ball of your foot or with your toe if you are wearing hard shoes. When kicking to the groin you may use the instep of the foot, coming straight up between the legs. The heel of the foot can also be used for a thrusting effect; this is particularly effective if you are wearing spike heels.

12

13. Roundhouse Kick Fold: Raise the knee as quickly as possible so that the side of the knee is parallel to the ground. Keep your arms close to your body for protection.

14. Roundhouse Kick: Snap the foot from the fold position horizontally to the target. As you complete the snap of the foot from the fold position, twist the hips for added power. Strike with the ball of the foot or the instep, or with the toe if you are wearing hard shoes.

13 14

15. Knee Strike: As with the elbow strike, the knee strike is used when you are too close to kick or punch. The groin is the primary target, but the solar plexus and even the face are possible targets if you can grasp the opponent and pull him into the strike. To deliver the strike, lift your knee up directly toward the target. Do not bend at the waist. Shoot the knee into the striking area and return it as quickly as possible.

15

16. Back Kick Fold: Make sure you see your target by looking over your shoulder above the leg that you plan to kick with. Lift your knee up into a cocked position as your arms remain in a defensive posture. Keep your standing leg slightly bent at the knee for balance.

17. Back Kick: Thrust the leg straight back, keeping your eyes on your opponent. Use the hip for added power, and keep the toes of your foot pointed toward the ground. Strike with the heel, and after contact retract the kick immediately into a defensive posture.

16   17

5
Blocks and Footwork

Beginning self-defense students often consider blocks and footwork exercises distasteful. These exercises lack the glamor and excitement of dramatic kicks and strikes. Beginners often fail to see the purpose of sometimes monotonous blocks and footwork drills.

In fact, blocks and footwork are easily as important as offensive strikes, just as a solid foundation is vital to the life of a house. And block and footwork exercises produce dramatic results, often in short time.

Blocks, of course, constitute the motions of redirecting or evading an enemy's strikes. Blocks rarely seek to stop a blow head-on. Instead, they redirect its force slightly, rendering it ineffective and paving the way for a counterattack. Repetition of blocking exercises has a way of seeping into the deeper levels of the mind, so that the student is soon blocking strikes automatically, even before he or she is consciously aware that the strikes have been thrown. It is a uniquely satisfying feeling to a student to discover that his or her body has reacted more swiftly than the conscious mind.

Good footwork is absolutely necessary to offensive strikes. It also allows the student to elude an attack deceptively, following immediately with a counterattack.

Here are drills that teach the student to block, evade, elude, and move in:

BLOCKS

1, 2. Center Block: Cross your left arm under your right arm while you twist your hip in the direction of the block. Immediately snap the left arm out to the front while keeping both hands in tight fists. Imagine an opponent throwing a punch as you block. Remember to stay relaxed until contact with the imaginary punch has been made. Repeat with the other side.

3, 4. Knife-Hand Block: Prepare to block an imaginary punch by bringing both arms back over your right shoulder with your palms facing your face. Stay relaxed as your elbows are bent in a cocked position. Immediately whip both arms forward to block, knocking the imaginary punch away with the left hand and guarding the solar plexus with the right. Remember to stay sideways throughout the block. Repeat with the other side.

5. Blocking a Kick: As your imaginary opponent attempts a roundhouse kick to your groin, pivot on your right foot as you lift your left knee to the block position. You will take the imaginary kick on the left shin as your right arm protects the solar plexus and your left arm reinforces the left leg block. Your left leg is now in position for a side-kick counterattack if necessary. Repeat with the other side.

6. Overhead Block: From the basic ready position raise your left arm as you block an imaginary punch to your face. Your right arm should be brought back to the ready position in order to prepare for a subsequent block or strike. Remember to stay relaxed through the course of the block until impact with the imaginary attacking punch. Block fast and hard.

5　　　　　　　　6

7, 8. Double Hand Block: From the ready position, with the hands open, turn to your right with the palms facing each other and your elbows bent at 90 degrees. After blocking the imaginary punch with your open hands, use your front hand to sweep the opponent's punch aside, and punch with your right hand. Let these two motions blend into one as you flow from the block to the counterattack. Stay relaxed until the counterpunch is completed. Repeat with the other side.

9. Reverse Strike Block: Starting with the left arm forward, palm facing upward, and elbow bent at 45 degrees, place the other hand behind your back with the back of your hand on your hips and your index finger, thumb, and forefinger pressed firmly together. From this position switch hands in a snapping semicircular fashion so that the right arm is forward and the left arm is back. Repeat with the other side.

7　　　　　　　8　　　　　　　9

10, 11. Downward Block of Center Punch: From the ready position, raise your right arm with the fist at eye level as you twist your hips in the direction of the block. Stay relaxed as you swing the arm down toward the midsection, blocking the imaginary strike. The arm swings down so that the elbow is bent at a 90-degree angle at about belt level. Repeat with the other side.

10

11

12, 13. Punching a Kick: Start with your right hand down in a fist with your arm extended, protecting your groin. Keep your left hand in a fist cocked under your left armpit. From this position thrust the left hand down as if punching a kick to the groin. Move the right hand to the cocked ready position. Remain relaxed through the duration of the technique until the actual completion when, for a split second, you focus your power into the block. Repeat with the other side.

12

13

14–17. Blocking a Punch-Kick: From the ready position, raise your right arm parallel to your face with your hand open as you block an imaginary punch to your head. Continue this hand's progression downward in a sweeping fashion in an attempt to block your imaginary opponent's kick to the body. While the arm is progressing downward, twist the hips into the block in order to protect your groin and add power to the block. Remain relaxed throughout the entire procedure until the blocking arm has swept the imginary punch and kick away. Repeat with the other side.

14

15

16

17

FOOT WORK

18-20. Shuffle: Start with your feet shoulder-width apart in a fighting stance. Keep your knees slightly bent, your back straight, and your blocking arms up. Replace your front foot with the rear foot, moving as quickly as possible. Attempt to "grab" the ground with your toes as you pull yourself forward. Remember to stay level by keeping your knees bent throughout the shuffle.

18　　　　　　　　　19　　　　　　　　　20

21. Jump: Start in a sparring position with your knees slightly bent and your back straight. Using your ankles and knees as a springboard, attempt to lunge forward and leap vertically in the same motion. Try not to telegraph the jump; stay relaxed and picture yourself as a cat pouncing on prey. Keep your arms close to your body and raise your knees for protection. Use the jump to cover a large distance when your opponent is on the defensive. A variety of strikes can be launched from the jumping position.

21

22, 23. Angular Stepping: From a sparring position, step with the rear foot at a 45-degree angle as if evading an attack from the front. Move quickly as you imagine yourself eluding the attack in a sliding motion. Immediately after taking the step, come back to your original position. Next use your other foot to step in the same manner.

22

23

24. Cross Step in front: From the sparring position, as quickly as possible bring the rear leg across in front of the front leg as you grab the floor with your toes and pull the leg across. Remember to keep your head at a uniform level throughout the move. Stay relaxed, moving smoothly. This is especially good for setting up a roundhouse kick as well as a variety of hand techniques.

24

25. Cross Step behind: As quickly as possible, bring your rear leg across behind the front leg, grabbing the floor with your toes. This is an excellent setup for a side kick.

25

26. Leaning: To evade an opponent's attack, simply lean back slightly, shifting the weight to the back leg. Prepare to counterattack immediately as an opening presents itself.

26

Another important technique, not pictured, is the push-slide. From the sparring position, raise your front leg while keeping your back as straight as possible. Keeping your guards up and your posture relaxed, let the act of lifting your leg actually drag you forward into your imaginary opponent. Remain level without jumping or rising, which can telegraph the movement.

6
Combinations

The progression from single techniques to combinations of techniques is vital. A single technique is rarely effective in sparring with a more experienced opponent. In an actual self-defense situation, a single technique without follow-up strikes can be disastrous.

Imagine you are confronted by an unarmed male assailant. The man is standing with his fists up. His groin is unprotected and you know exactly what you wish to do: You hurl a roundhouse kick straight to his groin, certain that this strike will leave him writhing on the ground. However, perhaps you miscalculate slightly, or perhaps he moves a bit just as you kick. The result is that your kick lands an inch or two high, enough to hurt but not devastate. While you wait for him to fall writhing to the ground, he springs on you in pained anger.

Now suppose you had followed your roundhouse kick with a back kick. The first kick, stunning him and moving him back, would have left him vulnerable to the second, more powerful strike. The back kick to the knee or groin would truly devastate him and leave him open for further attacks, such as an eye-jab or a palm-heel strike to the face.

Even if the initial roundhouse kick had worked, nothing would have been lost by follow-up techniques. In fact, the chances of disabling your attacker would have increased.

Do not stop with a single technique. Even if your initial technique is the most powerful strike in your repertoire, follow-up strikes can at least serve as insurance and at best can mean survival.

Combinations may also serve strategic purposes, particularly when taking on a wary or experienced opponent. A good fighter may be fast enough to block your initial technique, so let his blocking reaction be his undoing. A front kick to the groin may draw his guards down, leaving his face vulnerable for a jab. A rapid flurry of techniques, such as a jab–reverse punch–hook punch combination may "blitz" your opponent so that at least one of your strikes scores.

There are a wide variety of combinations that have proven to be effective. By practicing and experimenting, a student can find the combinations that work best for him or her.

Here is a sampling of combinations:

1, 2. Front Kick-Jab: From the sparring position, immediately snap the front kick into the knee or groin of your opponent. Allow your hands to remain in position for counterattack if necessary. As soon as the kick hits the target, follow up with a jab punch off the same side as the leg you used for kicking. Surprise is the key. Hit fast and hard without telegraphing your intentions.

1   2

3. Front Kick-Double Punch: Following the jab above, immediately throw a powerful reverse punch with the other hand. There should be virtually no time between these two strikes. The second punch should use the hip for added power.

3

4-6. Jab-Reverse Punch-Roundhouse Kick: Throw a front hand jab in order to create an opening for your powerful reverse punch. Make sure that the initial jab is effective in case your opponent fails to block it. Target the solid reverse punch toward an open area. If the opponent blocks both of these punches, cock your leg for a speedy roundhouse kick to the open target area. When throwing these techniques always follow up immediately, keeping the arms up in a defensive posture.

4　　　　　　5　　　　　　6

7-9. Defensive Side Kick-Jab-Punch: As your opponent moves toward you within kicking range, immediately strike with a side kick. This technique will halt his forward progress enough for you to counter with a jab followed by a reverse punch. Throw each technique in succession. Remember to use proper timing by striking only when the opponent is within range.

7　　　　　　8　　　　　　9

10-12. Shuffle Roundhouse Kick-Jab-Punch: From the sparring position, in order to close the gap between you and your opponent, execute a shuffle by replacing the front foot with the back foot, and immediately throw a front leg roundhouse kick. As the roundhouse kick is retracted, be prepared to hit with a front hand jab as soon as your foot is on the ground. Follow the jab with a powerful reverse punch.

10 11 12

13, 14. Jab-Shuffle Side Kick: Use a jab to close the distance between you and your opponent. Flick the jab out as quickly as possible to set up your powerful side kick. Drive the kick out quickly and explosively into the midsection of your opponent. Practice this combination until it is so fast that, if the opponent blocks the jab, there is no way for him to block the kick.

13 14

15–17. Jab-Reverse Punch–Hook Punch: When your opponent is too close to kick, throw a flicking jab to put him off guard. Immediately follow up with a reverse punch. After the reverse punch, twist your hips to give power to your hook punch. Use the first two knuckles of the fist for all three punches.

15 16 17

18, 19. Knife-Hand Strike–Side Kick: Use your rear hand to throw a knife-hand strike. Twist your hip with the motion and, as you strike to your opponent's neck, pivot your body so that you are in position for a rear leg side kick. Hit the body with the side kick, thrusting through the target area.

18 19

20-22. Reverse Punch-Side Kick-Reverse Punch: Throw a defensive reverse punch in order to stop your opponent's forward progress. Follow immediately with a rear leg side kick, hitting hard and fast. Finish your opponent by striking with another powerful reverse punch as you twist your hip for extra power.

20   21   22

23, 24. Roundhouse Kick-Back Kick: Throw a rear leg roundhouse kick hard and fast, hitting your opponent anywhere. This technique causes your opponent to move back so that you may have room to explode with a devastating back kick. Remember to keep your eyes on your opponent during each kick.

23   24

25, 26. Roundhouse Kick–Spinning Backfist: Throw a rear leg roundhouse kick in order to throw your opponent off balance. Immediately continue your spin into a backfist so that the power of the spin culminates in a whipping backfist strike to your opponent's head.

25

26

7
Sparring

Some students make the mistake of assuming that sparring is meant to simulate a self-defense encounter. Of course, it does not. Sparring consists basically of two students wearing protective pads squaring off for a light- to medium-contact bout in a ring. They attempt to confine their fighting to the ring, and numerous rules restrict their techniques. Although rules vary from one instructor to another, they are basically designed to prevent students from injuring one another. For instance, strikes to the legs, eyes, and back are prohibited, as is the use of knees and elbows.

Clearly, no such rules prevail in a genuine self-defense encounter. However, sparring teaches students many things that can be useful in an actual encounter. During sparring a student improves on blocks, footwork, and striking abilities. The student perfects timing, learning just when to strike, block, and move. The student learns which techniques best suit him or her. The student learns to take strikes—to experience the feeling of blows to the body—in a controlled environment, and the student gains confidence, learning that he or she can stand up and face an opponent in a combative situation.

Many other benefits come from sparring, such as speed, stamina, coordination, balance, and wariness. Here are some techniques, combinations, and guidelines to keep in mind while improving sparring performance:

1. Sparring Position: Probably no two students have identical sparring positions, but effective sparring stances have a number of things in common. Hands should be up to protect the head, with elbows tucked to guard the body. The body is turned partially or completely sideways to decrease open target areas. The back is straight, and knees are bent as the fighter maintains an agile stance for quick movement. Eyes are focused on the opponent's chest or midsection, not his face, in order to encompass movements of both hands and feet. Muscles remain relaxed until the moment of impact, thereby increasing speed and flexibility as well as reducing energy loss.

2. Body Work: (Purpose—to develop timing and confidence in the ability to take a punch or kick to different body areas.) Stand in a sparring position with your arms raised while your partner punches to different areas of your abdomen and chest. The intensity of these punches should be light so that you can spontaneously tighten and relax in the area your partner is punching. Remain relaxed between punches, tightening only when a punch makes contact. Learn to react instantaneously.

3. Kick Without Hip: (Purpose—to score on your opponent quickly in a snapping fashion, or to set the stage for a more powerful strike.) Kicking without the hip should be quick and controlled. Do not attempt to thrust through the target; instead, snap the technique at contact. Kicking without the hip is valuable in setting up a more powerful technique. This type of kick may be compared with a flicking jab in boxing. A snapping kick may be followed by a kick in which the hip is used in a thrusting fashion. Attempt to keep your back as straight as possible so as not to telegraph the kick.

1

2

3

4. Kick With the Hip: (Purpose—to generate as much power as possible by twisting the hip simultaneously with contact.) Kicking with the hip should be done in a thrusting motion and is devastating. The hip should be twisted into the technique a moment before impact so that maximum power may be realized. In all kicks in which the hip is used, it is a good idea to pivot on the supporting foot at the same instant when you thrust the hip. Keep the back straight; bending the back just prior to the kick can telegraph your intentions to a savvy opponent.

5. Angular Attack: (Purpose—to strike your opponent from an unexpected angle.) Rather than kicking from the same angle time after time, it is a good idea to vary the direction of the attack. For example, rather than shuffling straight in, move at a 45-degree angle to your opponent, forcing a different body angle to be exposed. Move quickly in order to take advantage of the opening, which may present itself for only a split second. Use this strategy sparingly in a match, because it becomes easy to counter eventually.

4 5

6-8. Feet Set Up Hands: (Purpose—to create an opening by directing your opponent's attention to your feet, enabling you to strike with your hand.) Use a kick to open up your opponent's guard so that you may strike with your hands. For example, you may attack your opponent with a front leg roundhouse kick to the head followed by a front hand attack. These attacks should proceed almost simultaneously so that the kick opens the door for the punch. Keep your defensive capabilities and awareness constantly in readiness in case you must block a counterattack.

6 7 8

9. Hands Set Up Feet: (Purpose—to create an opening by directing your opponent's attention to your hands, enabling you to score with a powerful kick.) Throw a front hand jab to open up your opponent's body for a kicking attack. As the front hand attacks the face of your opponent, he will either defend against the attack or get hit. If he defends by lifting his blocking hand, he opens up his body to the front kick. Make your initial hand strike effective in the event that he does not block it. Keep your arms in close to your body for defensive purposes. Fold the knee as high and as compactly as possible.

10-14. Lift the Knee to Set Up Three Kicks (roundhouse, side, hook): (Purpose—to use a single fold from which to strike your opponent from any of three angles, allowing for maximum deceptiveness.) The first step is to close the gap and lift the knee as high as possible in order to set up your opponent. When the knee threatens your opponent, he may react in an attempt to block. As he reacts, you must spontaneously see and then deliver the technique to the open target. The roundhouse kick may be delivered to the frontal area, the side kick to the lateral area, and the hook kick to the back area. The kicks may be used in any combination. Each of these kicks must be performed as quickly as possible once the target has been designated. A hook kick is thrown opposite from a roundhouse, striking with the heel. The power in all these kicks comes from snapping the knee as well as twisting the hips. Furthermore, if the knee is up at its maximum height, you can always drop it down as needed to strike a lower target on the body.

9

10

11

12

13

14

15, 16. Double Roundhouse Kick: (Purpose—to strike two different target areas with the same leg; the first kick stuns, the second devastates.) Start with your left side forward in a fighting position. Use a shuffle or push-slide in order to close the gap as you attack with a front leg roundhouse kick to the groin. If your opponent does not block this technique, you have scored a debilitating blow. However, if your opponent does block this kick, immediately cock the knee up and fire a high roundhouse kick to the face. Keep your back as straight as possible, with your arms in position to defend and strike out.

17. Jamming and Countering with a Punch: (Purpose—to block and strike simultaneously as quickly and efficiently as possible.) As your opponent attempts a backfist to your face, move inside with your forward hand blocking as you counter with a powerful rear-hand punch. Hit hard to the body and keep your hip in close to your opponent. Be ready to follow up with other hand techniques. Following this counterattack, either move in close or move back out of range of your opponent's attack. There must be no hesitation as you move in to jam. Commit yourself and be prepared to counter.

15

16

17

Note: Remember to respect your sparring partner, letting classroom sparring serve as a learning experience rather than a highly competitive encounter.

8
Grabs and Holds

An opponent who grabs you often has a false sense of security: He believes that by grasping you he has established dominance over you, ensuring your helpless submission. A person trained in self-defense, however, knows that there are many effective techniques for eluding or escaping virtually any hold or grab and rendering the assailant incapable of continuing his assault. Here are some principles to remember when confronted by an opponent who seeks to grab or hold you:

- Use your opponent's strength against him if possible. For example, instead of jerking directly against a wrist grab, move into your opponent with a strike so that his force actually gives power to your technique.
- Attempt to deliver a counterattack before your opponent secures his hold.
- Do not necessarily overreact to an attack. For example, rather than kicking and screaming, use your sense of relaxed alertness to deliver a blow to a target area.
- Use your weapons—arms, legs, knees, elbows, fingers, hips, forehead, feet—don't give up just because you seem to be overpowered.
- Practice the following techniques with a partner so that they become second nature.
- Always attack vital areas.
- Develop a sense of confidence and aggressive instinct that may be tapped at a moment's notice.

Here are some techniques to be used against grabs and holds:

1. Defense Against Wrist Grab: When an attacker grabs your wrist and pulls, immediately let that be your cue to use the momentum to deliver a solid punch. Your opponent's force will help you and be turned against him. To release your arm from such a hold, thrust explosively upward against the weak part of the grip—the thumb. This must be done so suddenly that the opponent does not have time to react by tightening his grip. Follow up with a kick or hand strike.

2. Defense Against Choke—Finger Thrust: If your opponent is attempting to secure you in a choke hold, strike fast and hard with rigid fingers to the throat, preferably to the hollow spot just below the Adam's apple, an especially vulnerable spot. Follow up with other techniques.

3. Defense Against Choke—Side Swipe: If an attacker has secured you in a choke hold, push suddenly on the inside of his forearms with your hands in a crosswise fashion. Because the attacker is applying pressure with his thumbs rather than with the sides of his hands, this simple gesture will nullify his attack. By the same token, jerking your neck suddenly backward can free you from the same grip, since his power is not focused in the fingers behind your neck. Follow up immediately with a knee to the groin.

1

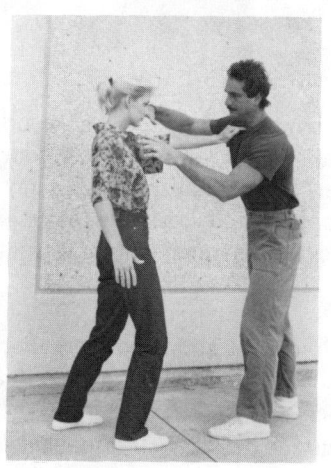
2

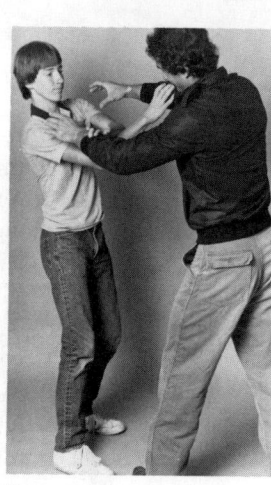
3

4. Defense Against Front Grab—Elbow to Solar Plexus: As the attacker grabs your lapel, let the momentum from his pull aid you in delivering maximum power with an elbow strike upward into the solar plexus. Follow up with a punch from the opposite hand.

5. Defense Against Front Bear Hug—Palm Smash to Ears: If an attacker manages to secure you in a front bear hug, use both of your hands in a clapping motion across the attackers' ears or temples. Follow up with a forehead strike to his nose.

6, 7. Defense Against Front Bear Hug (over arms)—Forehead Smash to Nose: If many of your bodily weapons are nullified, don't forget your forehead. Just on the hairline is a hard spot that may be used as a bludgeon on an attacker's nose. Hit fast and hard, using a follow-up technique if needed.

8. Defense Against Rear Hold—Hammerfist to Groin: If an attacker grabs you from behind, immediately shift your hips to one side, exposing your attacker's groin. Use the base of the fist like a hammer to strike to the groin.

CHAPTER 8 GRABS AND HOLDS

9. Defense Against Rear Hold—Shin Rake: If an attacker grabs you from behind, look down and see your attacker's shin as a target. Strike explosively to the shin with the heel of your shoe. Follow up with other techniques.

10. Defense Against Rear Hold—Instep Stomp: If grabbed from behind, your first objective is to loosen your opponent's hold. Stomp down fast and hard with your heel onto your opponent's instep, a weak area that can be crushed relatively easily. Use follow-up techniques such as a hammerfist to the groin.

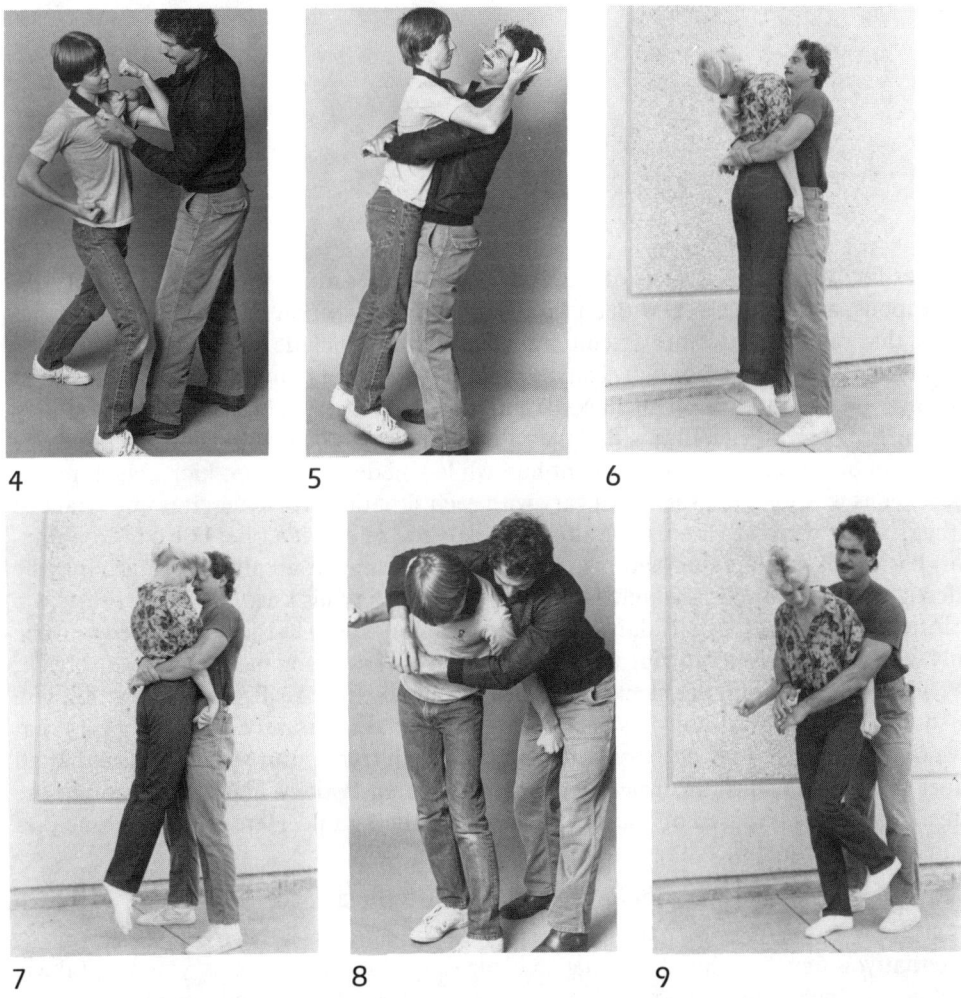

4 5 6

7 8 9

9 Weapons

This chapter focuses on two aspects of weapons: how to use ordinary, readily accessible objects as weapons, and how to deal with an assailant bearing a weapon such as a knife or gun.

Objects that can be turned into extemporaneous weapons include keys, pencils, nail files, purses, cans of soft drinks, umbrellas, chairs, brooms—just about anything that's handy and that may increase your odds in a violent confrontation. Keys inserted between the fingers may render a punch far more effective; a nail file to the temple can be deadly; soft drink can be thrown into an opponent's face to disorient him while you deliver a front kick. The types of extemporaneous weapons and their uses vary with each situation. However, it is important to realize that such a "weapon" is only one alternative: do not rely on it alone! Use it in combination with basic strikes and combinations. A broomstick swung at an attacker's face may be most effective when followed up immediately with a side kick to his knee.

An armed attacker is especially dangerous, and techniques such as those presented must be used only with great discretion owing to the risk involved. If a person has a gun at your back, you may wish to use the spinning block shown below, but you must realize that if you fail, you may be shot. Is the risk absolutely necessary? Are there other alternatives? If it appears that you have only seconds to live, any technique may be worth trying. But we emphasize that all techniques to be used against an armed opponent are extremely risky, and the decision to use such a technique must be based on the circumstances of the assault. Here are some principles to keep in mind regarding such a situation:

- Use active resistance against a weapon only if your life is threatened.
- Never attack the weapon; attack the man.
- Realize that you may be injured in order to come out alive. For example, you may take a knife wound in the forearm in order to subdue the attacker. This is called a **sacrifice**.
- Develop a philosophy that will allow you to react spontaneously in an unafraid manner if confronted with a weapon.
- Wait until the most opportune moment to unleash your attack. You may wish to wait until your assailant seems momentarily careless or off guard.

CHAPTER 9 WEAPONS **51**

- When all other passive resistance techniques are fruitless, then and only then use active resistance against an armed attacker.
- If you do decide to use active resistance, do not hesitate! Give it all you've got. Remember that your attacker plans to do you serious harm.

Here are some examples for using extemporaneous weapons:

1. Keys: If you are in an area where you suspect you might be subject to assault, secure your keys in your hand so that they protrude between the fingers. If attacked, use the keys to complement your punching action to the eyes of the attacker. Use a raking action, throwing a hook punch across the attacker's face.

2. Soft Drink Can: If you are carrying a soft drink, slosh the liquid or throw the can itself into the opponent's face. Follow up immediately with a kick to the groin while he is distracted.

3. Nail File: Use a nail file (or any hard, pointed object) to strike an attacker if he attempts to grab you from behind. The file may also be used to strike to the temple or eye. Do not forget the principles of self-defense when using such a weapon; be ready to use other techniques, blocks, and footwork, just as you would if you did not have the file.

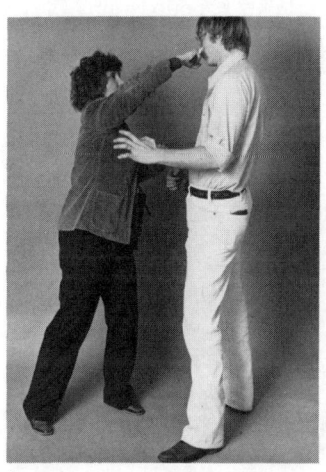

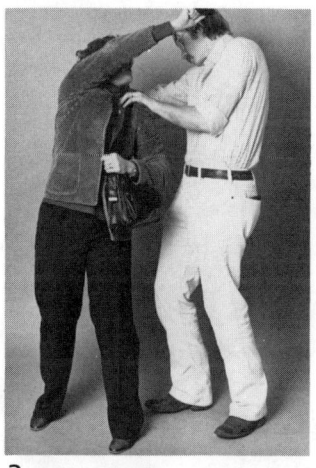

1 2 3

4. Purse: The purse is a "weapon" that nearly all women carry. Use it to distract your opponent while you follow up with your keychain to a vital area. Striking with the purse will automatically bring your opponent's hands to his face, leaving his groin exposed.

Here are some techniques that may be used against an opponent armed with knife or gun:

5. Defense Against Knife—Side Kick: If an attacker threatens you with a knife, lean so that your body is out of range of the knife and deliver a side kick to the attacker's knee. If you succeed in causing damage to the knee, run away.

52 CHAPTER 9 WEAPONS

4

5

6, 7. Defense Against Knife—Block and Palm-Heel: If the attacker thrusts at you with the knife, you may attempt to deflect his wrist. However, be prepared to take a cut on the arm in order that you may deliver a powerful blow to a vital area, such as a palm-heel to the groin. The same principles apply if the opponent holds his knife in front of him within your reach.

6

7

8–11. Defense Against Gun: If an attacker has a gun held to your back and he appears to be taking you out to be shot, your only alternative may be to wait for the right moment to strike. Make sure you see which hand holds the gun (**9**). Next, pivot and use your elbow to deflect the gun **(10)**. If you do this suddenly, he may not have time to react and pull the trigger. Immediately counterattack with your fingers to his eyes **(11)**, thrusting them deep into the sockets.

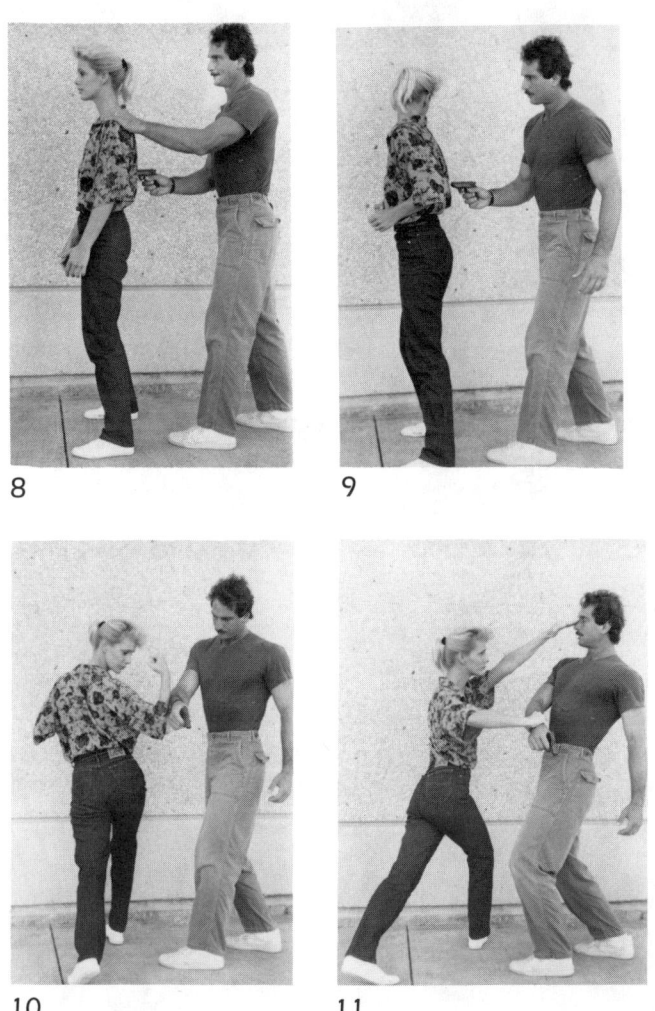

12-14. Defense Against Gun—Frontal Attack: If the attacker seems about to shoot you, you may be forced to attempt to deflect the gun to the side. Act quickly and precisely as you secure the gun in preparation for a follow-up **(13)**. Thrust your knee into your opponent's groin **(14)**.

CHAPTER 9 WEAPONS

12   13   14

Note: Again we wish to point out that such techniques should be attempted only in the most desperate of circumstances.

10
Home Practice

A variety of techniques can be practiced at home, with a minimum of equipment or assistance, to increase flexibility, physical condition, and fighting techniques. Only a small space is needed. Here is a sampling of simple exercises that may be practiced at home in your spare time:

1. Front Wall Stretch: (Purpose—to stretch the hamstring and calf muscles of each leg with the ultimate goal of improving the front kick.) Stand with your back against the wall, erect, with your feet together and your knees straight. Extend your right leg so that your partner can grab your ankle. Let your partner slowly push up against the back of the heel until you feel tension in the hamstring. At the point of tension, tell your partner to stop and hold that position. Hold for three seconds and then have your partner slowly bring your leg back down to the floor. Remember to keep your muscles relaxed and to maintain correct form throughout the stretch. Switch sides and perform the same routine with your other leg.

2. Side Wall Stretch: (Purpose—to improve flexibility in the groin muscles in order to enhance performance of the side kick, roundhouse kick, and hook kick.) Stand facing

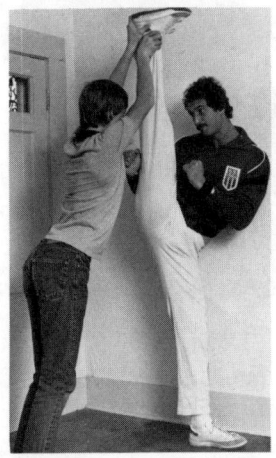

1   2

sideways to the wall with your feet together and your knees straight. Extend your outside leg directly to the side so that your foot is parallel to the floor. Let your partner grab your ankle and slowly raise your leg until it reaches the point of tension. Hold for three seconds. Let your partner slowly lower your leg to the floor. Remember to remain relaxed throughout the routine. Repeat with your other leg.

3. Knee Wall Stretch: (Purpose—to improve hip and hamstring flexibility, enhancing ability to cock leg for kicks.) Stand with your back against the wall. Raise your leg as high as you can with your knee bent. Have your partner push on the bottom of your foot with your knee at a 90-degree angle so that the knee is directed toward the wall. Have your partner push slowly until you feel tension in the hip. Hold for three seconds, maintaining an erect, relaxed posture. After your leg is lowered slowly to the floor, repeat with the other leg.

4. Lean Front Stretch: (Purpose—to improve flexibility of the hamstrings in both legs.) Stand with your left leg against the wall and let your partner grab your right ankle. Keep both legs straight as your partner places your foot on his or her shoulder. Your partner gradually walks backward until tension is reached. Hold for three seconds, and then have your partner slowly set your foot back down. Repeat with the other leg.

5. Lean Side Stretch: (Purpose—to improve flexibility in groin muscles.) Stand with your left side against the wall. Keep both knees straight as you extend your right leg to your partner, who will put your foot on his or her shoulder and slowly begin to walk backward until you reach a point of tension. Hold for three seconds; replace foot to floor and repeat with the other leg.

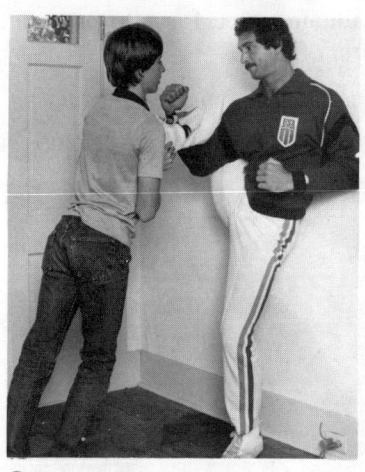

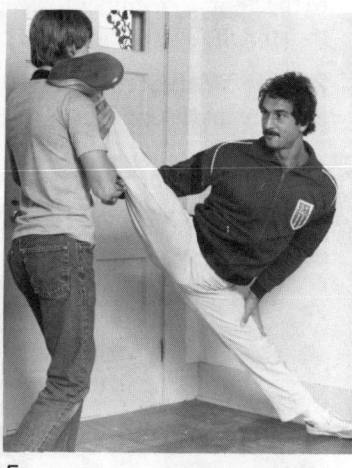

3   4   5

6. Target Kicking: (Purpose—to improve control of kicking and punching techniques to specific targets.) Sometimes it is a good idea to hang up a target such as tissue paper, a ball on a string, or some other object, to be used as a practice target for kicking accuracy. If your partner holds the target for you, have him or her vary its height and distance in order to create a more realistic setting. Hit fast and retract the technique quickly. Think about controlling your angle of attack.

7, 8. Mirror Practice: (Purpose—to practice new strategies as well as train on weaknesses that need correcting.) Use the mirror to see whether you are executing techniques correctly. Watch for problematic telegraphing of techniques as well as lack of flow in performance. Pay attention to angle, speed, control, form, and posture. Use the mirror to discover your strong techniques.

9-13. Weight Training: (Purpose—to gain strength, muscular endurance, and confidence in order to improve fighting ability.) Weight training is a terrific form of exercise, strengthening cartilaginous and muscular tissue. Increasing the strength of the muscles may aid your ability to take a punch as well as the power of your strikes. Lift only enough weight so that you can perform at least ten repetitions. Always perform each exercise through the full range of motion. Breathe normally as you perform the exercises unless you are having trouble lifting the weight. If it is difficult, exhale on each repetition for added power. Remember that if you work out a certain body part, the "specificity of training rule" is in effect, whereby only that particular area will be improved.

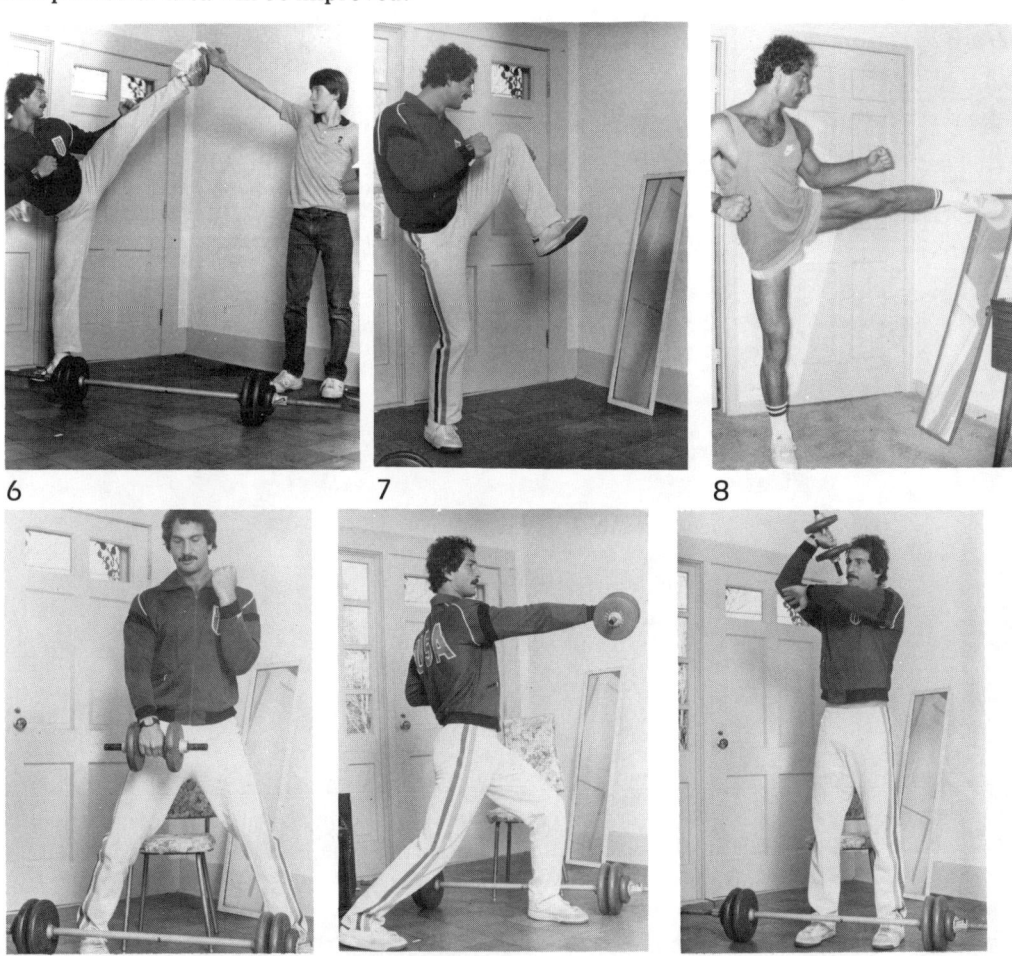

6
7
8

9
10
11

CHAPTER 10 HOME PRACTICE

12

13

PART THREE
Cognitive Strategies

11
Ancient Wisdom

Many of us feel that we cannot perform up to our potential because we have not learned the ancient oriental techniques of self-mastery. For example, in order for a mind to be "still like water," or to "focus our chi" (internal power), we must be trained as monks in a Chinese Shaolin temple for half a lifetime—correct? We used to think so! It took one of us (Seabourne) ten years of studying Eastern philosophy and analyzing it in Western terms finally to develop simple psychological techniques that ultimately aided in winning the U.S. Tae Kwon Do Karate Championships and finishing as a finalist in the World Games.

This study took place in Okinawa, Japan and Taiwan and encompassed as much as possible of traditional meditation (i.e., traditional and Zen Buddhism, yoga), focus of chi, and a search for that elusive inner strength. These techniques, if practiced correctly, are useful, but many Westerners do not have the time or cultural background for this type of training.

There are numerous easily learned techniques available to you: simple step-by-step procedures that are indeed a shortcut compared with many of the Eastern approaches to training. Bear in mind that these psychological techniques do take practice, but the results can be yours without a cultural translation.

Whether you learn such techniques from modern scientific researchers or at the feet of an ascetic monk, the principles are essentially the same as they have been for thousands of years. These principles point out that although physical training is of immeasurable importance, the other side of the coin—development of inner strength—is also of great importance. Oriental legends are rich in accounts of frail little monks who, because of their tremendous inner power, easily thwarted the energetic and superbly trained fighters of their day. Consider these words from the *Tao Tê Ching,* written some 2,500 years ago:

> He who is filled with virtue is like a newborn child.
> Wasps and serpents will not sting him;
> Wild beasts will not pounce upon him;
> He will not be attacked by birds of prey.
> His bones are soft, his muscles weak,
> But his grip is firm.

This suggests that inner stability is even more important than physical preparedness.

We certainly do not advocate setting physical weakness as your goal, and we do not think that Lao-Tsu, the writer of the *Tao Tê Ching,* does either. But who has not noticed the common traits among beginning fighters of tremendous expenditure of energy that brings little or no results, erratic breathing, and lack of control? Physical energy and strength without the balancing forces of inner stability and power can actually be self-defeating. Consider what the above writing goes on to say:

It is not wise to rush about.
Controlling the breath causes strain.
If too much energy is used, exhaustion follows.
This is not the way of Tao.
Whatever is contrary to Tao will not last long.

Physical strength and energy on their own are unstable. Consider the forces that affect them: age, health, diet, emotions, fatigue. Without an underlying inner strength to nourish them, they may be pathetically ephemeral. Physical strength and energy allow one to endure and to sustain powerful assaults. Inner strength allows one to master a situation, even when the opponent appears to possess a greater store of physical strength and energy.

Physical ability and mental power are an unbeatable combination. The person who steps into the street in peak physical condition and with a mind that is alert, relaxed, and poised is a formidable opponent indeed.

12
An Overview

Psychological strategies and mental preparations are important in enhancing one's potential to the maximum. In a self-defense situation, a person who is proficient in fighting skills but lacking in mental preparedness may be at a disadvantage. Those who realize their physical limitations may learn to divert more attention to the development of psychological skills. They will learn that both mental and physical processes must work together to perform effectively. In order for the mind and body to work together effectively, individuals learn to cope with any excess anxiety caused by the pressures of living in a sometimes hostile environment.

Over the past several years, a variety of cognitive techniques (e.g., transcendental meditation, biofeedback, autogenic training, and progressive relaxation) have been used in trying to cope with the excessive anxiety brought about by stressful situations. Although these techniques differ, they all attempt to bring about the **relaxation response,** which is characterized by steadier breathing, heart rate, and blood pressure; by relaxed muscles; and often by clearer, more dispassionate thinking. The general trend seems to indicate that the practice of these mental techniques can improve such necessary factors as alertness, attention, and reaction time. In a street situation, the ability to control anxiety and keep your excitement at an optimal level can greatly improve the chances that your self-defense techniques will be effective.

One important cognitive strategy used to improve physical performance is **mental imagery.** Imagery can be broken down into two types: external and internal. External imagery means envisioning your performance from the perspective of a spectator. It is as if you were watching a movie of yourself in action.

The internal type of imagery consists of visualizing performance from your own perspective. Internal visualization has been deemed by some to be more valuable in improving physical performance. It consists of developing a clear mental picture of the performance situation and then imagining how it feels to perform optimally. Mental imagery may be helpful in many ways. You may visualize yourself practicing basic strikes effectively in order to improve your techniques; you may imagine a classroom sparring situation in which you perform skillfully and accurately; or you may imagine an actual street situation in order to prepare your mind for the high stress involved there and to imagine using your self-defense techniques in a genuinely threatening encounter.

Internal visualization has come naturally to many top athletes. Fran Tarkenton, statistically the all-time leading passer in the National Football League, says he visualizes most aspects of an upcoming game. Another top athlete, Bruce Jenner, said he used mental imagery to rehearse every event while training for his 1976 Olympic decathlon victory.

A combination of a relaxation technique plus imagery termed **visuo-motor behavior rehearsal** (VMBR) has been receiving increased attention as another cognitive method to improve performance. The technique has two phases. The initial phase of VMBR is designed to induce relaxation. The second phase involves practicing internal mental imagery of the impending stressful situation. Case studies have indicated that VMBR training can be used effectively in performance events.

One researcher taught VMBR to Alpine skiers, whose performance immediately improved. Case studies also indicate that an athlete can use VMBR to prepare for a new and difficult maneuver. A gymnast, for instance, could use VMBR training to become mentally acclimated to a new trick before attempting it physically. A self-defense student might use VMBR to imagine using techniques in a situation that cannot be safely or realistically practiced in a classroom situation.

A number of individuals have felt that the use of cognitive techniques has improved their ability to handle their chosen tasks. Such techniques can thus be seen as an important factor in overall training.

13
The Jitters

As Lao-Tsu writes, "People usually fail when they are on the verge of success." Why is this? It is because of the jitters—anxiety.

To cope with anxiety, most individuals have a particular method of mentally preparing for an upcoming situation that promises to be stressful. Perhaps a person has no method at all to cope with the jitters. What apparently makes the situation worse is the realization that anxiety itself can affect the performance of even the most skillful individual, just as a person fluent in party conversation may totally freeze up with stage fright in front of a large, formal audience. The anxiety associated with street self-defense situations, or even with classroom sparring sessions, is especially significant to the individual who may feel unable to perform at full potential because of nervous panic.

Although too much anxiety may actually impair physical performance, there appears to be a certain level of anxiety or "arousal" necessary for an individual to perform to his or her potential. The Inverted U Hypothesis addresses the notion that there is an optimal level of arousal at which maximum performance results. In other words, too little arousal may be as damaging as too much. Somewhere between complete calm and intense arousal with the tremble of jittery nerves lies a perfect medium toward which the individual should strive.

Studies show that this perfect arousal level differs not only for each person, but also for each task or pursuit. Activities that require a lot of speed, strength, or endurance but little complexity or fine muscle control require a high degree of arousal. These may include such activities as blocking in football, lifting weights, swimming in races, and performing the running long jump.

Activities requiring mostly fine muscle control, precision, and coordinated movements require a lower level of arousal for maximum performance. These may include tennis, golf, archery, and bowling. Mid-level pursuits include basketball and gymnastics. Martial arts activities may require high or low levels of arousal depending on the situation and the particular skill involved. Clearly, individuals need to be aware of techniques whereby they can effectively manage their levels of anxiety and find that level of arousal that best suits them and the situations they expect to encounter.

The high-intensity situation of a street assault is likely to find an individual laden with more anxiety than necessary. The person in this situation may need to know how to lower his or her anxiety or arousal rather than increase it.

Many different cognitive strategies may be used for controlling anxiety. Any of these techniques, if used properly, may bring about the relaxation response that can have such a great impact on the way in which you respond to a dangerous situation.

14
Finding the Right Level

The relaxation response can be elicited with an effortless and comfortable mental technique developed by Herbert Benson to be practiced for twenty minutes in the morning and twenty minutes in the evening. Think of a sound and repeat it in your mind for the twenty-minute period. That sound eventually disappears, and your mind will experience more subtle levels of thought, arriving at a very low level of arousal. At the end of the twenty minutes, much of your body's tension will have been released and you will feel refreshed and ready for action.

The requirements needed for the practice of the relaxation technique include a comfortable posture; a quiet environment; a passive mental attitude (a willingness to let random thoughts pass through your mind without disrupting the practice of the technique); and a constant word, sound, or image repeated over and over to minimize your attention to distractions.

This and similar techniques have proven to be popular and successful methods of achieving deep relaxation. Among the aims of the relaxation response are the development of an increased ability to focus and maintain awareness and the improvement of sensitivity toward your own inner goings-on. The benefits commonly attributed to this relatively simple method of meditation are numerous. Many individuals, for example, claim to become more alert, develop better concentration, become better able to resist stress, and enjoy increased consistency in performance. Greater alertness may translate into faster reaction time. All of these characteristics point toward increased confidence and descreased fear and stress.

However, there are two sides to the relaxation coin. On the one hand, relaxed but alert individuals may be better able to handle their chosen tasks, as in the case of some shot-putters studied who performed better after using relaxation techniques. But consider the state of a very tense boxer at the Mexico City Olympic Games who used mental techniques to reduce anxiety. He was successful in reducing his anxiety, all right. The problem was that he came out smiling, with his arms down to his side, causing him to be knocked out early in the first round. Clearly this athlete failed to find the correct level of arousal for himself and his situation and wound up with too little anxiety.

Biofeedback is another technique that can induce relaxation. In one study involving archers, it was shown that through biofeedback training muscle tension levels were significantly reduced. However, there was no apparent increase in the archers' performance. Why? Evidently relaxed muscles were not what was needed for the archers to shoot better.

Mental imagery, which has been discussed earlier, is used by many individuals to improve performance. Internal imagery seems particularly helpful. It has been suggested by researchers that when performers use internal imagery they actually transmit neural impulses from the brain to the muscles. In other words, the nervous system appears to send out electrical currents to the body cells comparable to those sent out in an actual physical workout. Such imagery conceivably could have a training effect on muscles, improving their coordination.

Although the physiological effects of imagery on the musculature are important, the vividness and controllability of the image may be significant variables in using the technique properly. **Vividness** concerns the clarity of the mental picture. A person may create a fuzzy, distorted image of his or her performance, providing an undesirable model. If the visual model is unrealistic or unclear, the beneficial feedback to the musculature may be eliminated. If the mental image is distorted, it becomes difficult for the brain to facilitate the transfer of impulses through the proper neuromuscular pathways.

Controllability refers to whether the image changes according to the person's intentions. In some case studies, it was shown that individuals had difficulty in controlling the image they intended to create. In one study with basketball players, several athletes reported that their images seemed almost uncooperative. In dribbling before a free throw, one player imagined that his basketball simply would not bounce.

Nevertheless, there are plenty of anecdotes about cases in which mental imagery has helped. Consider Robert Foster, a former national rifle champion who was called to Vietnam in a noncombat capacity. While there, he mentally rehearsed rifle shooting ten minutes a day for the year that he was away. Upon his return to the United States, with little practice he entered a national meet and broke his own world record.

Champion golfer Jack Nicklaus says that his good shots are ten percent swing, forty percent set-up and stance, and fifty percent mental picture. He describes this visualization practice: "I never hit a shot, not even in practice, without having a very sharp, in-focus picture of it in my head. It's like a color movie."

Mental imagery can play an important part in the acquisition and improvement of self-defense skills. The practice of basic strikes, combinations, sparring, and other aspects of self-defense training can be enhanced by the proper use of mental imagery. Relaxation and imagery techniques, along with suggestions given to enhance confidence, fearlessness, balance, and other desirable attributes, can enable better preparation for a street conflict.

15
Relaxation and Imagery: VMBR

Some researchers contend that relaxation-based techniques or imagery practice alone is not as effective as the combination of relaxation and imagery. As we have seen, relaxation techniques work toward reducing anxiety before a stressful situation, while mental imagery is used to enhance performance levels.

Suinn argues that the combination of relaxation and imagery, termed **visuo-motor behavior rehearsal** (VMBR), seems particularly useful for anxiety control. The technique involves an initial relaxation phase in which the individual relaxes himself or herself both physically and mentally. This is followed by an imagery phase in which the person visualizes his or her performance during a specific stressful situation. For example, you may see yourself walking down a deserted alley physically and mentally prepared for an impending confrontation.

VMBR has also been used to enhance transfer of the motor skills from practice to actual situations. VMBR experiences are so realistic that they enable the person to practice performing under conditions nearly comparable to the real thing. Not only do the experiences seem realistic, they may be realistically interpreted neuromuscularly, as noted in Chapter 14. Through the use of electromyographic equipment, recordings were obtained from the leg muscles of a skier during a VMBR session. The recordings showed several spurts of muscle activity, suggesting that the nervous system was sending out electrical currents through body cells, facilitating the coordination of neural and muscular activity. Comparably, self-defense students may find themselves blocking or striking imaginary opponents while they are in a state of deep relaxation just before sleep.

Another use of VMBR is to practice for the unexpected. In one study, it was shown that the difference between successful Olympic tryout competitors and those who did not win a position on the team depended on their responses to errors. The successful ones used the error as a cue for what needed to be done next, rather than as a source of distraction from the routine. VMBR has been used with the statement, "In a moment, something unexpected will happen," in order to have the individual mentally practice quick adjustments to changing circumstances. A self-defense student may use VMBR to go mentally through a variety of unexpected situations that may occur in the classroom or in the street.

VMBR has also been applied as a diagnostic method. Occasionally, neither an instructor nor a student can determine what went wrong during a specific situation. For instance, when an "attacker" overcomes his "victim" during classroom practice—or, conceivably, even during a real-life attack—VMBR can be used to repeat the scene with instructions to pay attention to what went wrong. It may then be possible to identify the flaw and correct it with another VMBR session.

VMBR subjects report feeling physical sensations during their VMBR sessions. A swimmer reports feeling the cold slap of the water, a skier reports the exhilaration and excitement of speeding over the slopes, and a self-defense student feels himself successfully blocking an attack.

With reference to street defense situations and sparring performance, Weinberg, Seabourne, and Jackson have conducted a number of studies testing the effects of cognitive strategies on performance. One study concerned the effects of relaxation and imagery. Results of this study showed that relaxation and imagery combined were more beneficial to sparring performance than was either relaxation training or imagery training alone.

Because these results imply that relaxation and imagery should be practiced together, a question remains as to how often a person should practice these techniques. Is a single exposure enough, or should a person practice relaxation and imagery on a daily basis?

The answer to this question was shown in the results of a subsequent study in which one group practiced relaxation–imagery for ten minutes daily over six weeks. This group improved its performance significantly over that of a group that practiced relaxation–imagery only on the first or final day of the same six-week session. Thus, daily practice of relaxation–imagery may be valuable to self-defense performance.

However, another valid question about relaxation–imagery practice concerns whether a group approach or an individual approach to training in the technique is more valuable. This question inspired a third study in which one group practiced and trained with an individual approach to relaxation–imagery while another group practiced with no individual training. A control group was added to the researchers' design. In the control group, the subjects meditated on quotations from early Chinese writings. Results of this study showed that the group with the individualized approach to the practice and training of relaxation–imagery had superior performance in single-skill techniques, combinations, and sparring.

In summary:

- Relaxation–imagery is more valuable to performance improvement than the practice of either relaxation or imagery alone.
- Relaxation–imagery should be practiced on a daily basis rather than just one time.
- The relaxation–imagery technique should be designed specifically for the individual in a practice-training approach.

16
The Path to Relaxation

Here is a look at a highly detailed method, developed by Jacobson, for producing the relaxation response:

1. Get as comfortable as possible. Tight clothing should be loosened; your legs should not be crossed. Take a deep breath, let it out slowly, and become as relaxed as possible.

2. Raise your arms and extend them out in front of you. Make a fist with both hands as hard as you can. Notice the uncomfortable tension in your hands and fingers. Hold the tension for five seconds, then let the tension out halfway and hold for an additional five seconds. Notice the decrease in tension, but also concentrate on the tension that is still present. Then let your hands relax completely. Notice how the tension and discomfort drain from your hands and are replaced by sensations of comfort and relaxation. Focus on the contrast between the tension you felt and the relaxation you now feel. Concentrate on relaxing your hands completely for ten to fifteen seconds.

3. Tense your upper arms hard for five seconds. Focus on the feeling of tension. Then let the tension out halfway for an additional five seconds. Again, focus on the tension that is still present. Now relax your upper arms completely for ten to fifteen seconds and focus carefully on the developing relaxation. Let your arms rest limply at your sides.

4. With your toes supported and your legs relaxed, dig the toes of your feet into the bottom of your shoes. After five seconds, relax the toes halfway and hold the reduced tension for an additional five seconds. Then relax your toes completely and focus on the relaxation spreading into the toes. Continue relaxing your toes for ten to fifteen seconds.

5. Point your toes downward so that the feet and calves are tensed. Hold the tension hard for five seconds, and then relax your feet and calves completely for ten to fifteen seconds.

6. Extend your legs and raise them approximately six inches above the floor and tense your thigh muscles. Hold the tension for five seconds, let it out halfway for an additional five seconds, and then relax your thighs completely. Concentrate on totally relaxing your feet, calves, and thighs for about thirty seconds.

7. Tense your buttock muscles hard for five seconds, then let the tension out halfway for another five seconds. Finally, relax your buttocks completely and focus on the sensations of heaviness and relaxation. Concentrate also on relaxing the other muscle groups with which you have already dealt.

8. Tense your stomach muscles as hard as possible for five seconds and concentrate on the tension. Then let the tension out halfway for an additional five seconds before relaxing your stomach muscles completely. Focus on the spreading relaxation until your stomach muscles are completely relaxed.

9. Press the palms of your hands together and push so as to tense the chest and shoulder muscles. Hold the tension for five seconds, then let the tension out halfway for an additional five seconds. Now relax the muscles completely and concentrate on the relaxation until they are completely relaxed.

10. Push your shoulders back as far as possible in order to tense your back muscles. Let the tension out halfway after five seconds, hold the reduced tension and focus on it carefully for an additional five seconds, and then relax your back and shoulder muscles completely. Focus on the spreading relaxation until these muscles are completely relaxed.

11. While keeping the muscles of your torso, arms, and legs relaxed, tense your neck muscles by bringing your head forward until your chin digs into your chest. Hold for five seconds, release the tension halfway for another five seconds, and then relax your neck completely. Allow your head to hang comfortably while you focus on the relaxation developing in your neck muscles.

12. Clench your teeth and notice the tension in the muscles of your jaws. After five seconds, let the tension out halfway for five seconds, and then relax completely. Let your mouth relax completely with your lips slightly parted and concentrate on totally relaxing these muscles for ten to fifteen seconds.

13. Tense your tongue by pushing it into the roof of your mouth as hard as possible. Hold for five seconds, then let the tension out halfway and hold for an additional five seconds before relaxing your tongue completely. Focus now on completely relaxing the muscles of your neck, jaw, and tongue.

14. With your eyes closed, squint and rotate your eyeballs upward as if you were looking up. Hold the tension for five seconds, then release it halfway for an additional five seconds. Relax your eyes completely. Focus on the relaxation developing in your eyes and concentrate on relaxing your other facial muscles.

15. Wrinkle your forehead and scalp as hard as possible. Hold the tension for five seconds, then release halfway for another five seconds. Relax your scalp and forehead completely, as always focusing on the developing feeling of relaxation and contrasting it with the tension which existed earlier. Concentrate for about a minute on relaxing all the muscles of your body.

16. Take a series of short inhalations, about one per second, until the chest is filled. Hold for about five seconds, then exhale slowly for about ten seconds while thinking silently to yourself the word *relax* or *calm*. Think or picture the word to yourself as you slowly let out

your breath. Repeat the process at least five times, each time striving to deepen the state of relaxation you are experiencing.

The deep controlled breathing is very important and should be practiced as frequently as possible. Research has shown that this type of breathing can quickly lower bodily arousal and tension. It is suggested that in subsequent relaxation practice sessions, the deep breathing exercise should be employed between each muscle-group exercise so as to deepen the state of relaxation and allow you to practice muscle relaxation in conjunction with deep breathing.

To practice the above relaxation technique, have someone read you the steps, or tape someone reading them and listen to the tape.

17
Concentration and "Flow"

Concentration is nothing more than focusing your complete and undivided attention on a chosen object or task and becoming absorbed in that object while excluding irrelevant internal factors (worry, self-doubt, distracting thoughts) as well as external ones (sounds, sights, distractions).

You concentrate best when you are relaxed. Thus relaxation and concentration are interrelated. The mind should be calm but focused, the body relaxed but ready. Relaxed concentration is a learned art that must be practiced to be perfected. If you become absorbed in the experience itself, success will take care of itself.

What is relaxed concentration?

- Attention is sharp, selective, and focused; power of anticipation is heightened.
- Interest is found in what you are doing; you become absorbed in your task.
- Your willpower is strong and undivided.

The question arises: what can be done before or during a self-defense situation to aid power of concentration?

If actions can be thought out ahead of time, a self-defense student will tend to make fewer mistakes during the situation in question. Visualization or controlled mental imagery is an exercise in positive thinking and can be used effectively to improve performance. Imagery is seeing and feeling yourself going through a perfect performance from your own point of view. However, you must see your mental image perform proper techniques and not allow the mental image to perform incorrectly. It is important to feel fully involved in the behavior being rehearsed rather than to "stand outside" yourself and merely watch yourself perform. When the experience seems real to you, take the image and feeling and convert them into physical practice.

For some practitioners, imagery serves as a last-minute reminder of the pattern they wish to reproduce. For others, it takes their minds off any thoughts of worry or self-doubt, reaffirming a last-second feeling of confidence.

Research indicates that ten minutes is the optimal amount of time to practice imagery. Ideally one should practice a relaxation technique for five minutes, followed by five minutes of mental imagery.

Concentration is an important ingredient in successful street defense experience, entailing total immersion or absorption in the particular act that you are performing. The feeling of concentrating fully, as in sparring or practicing basic strikes, can be exhilarating. You do not know you are in a state of concentration until you come out of it, because while you are in it you are totally absorbed by the proper things you should be doing and not distracted by internal or external interference. If you lose your concentration, simply become aware of your arousal level—too low? too high?—as well as where the focus of your attention lies. In order for the mind and body to be in harmony in any performance situation, you must synchronize the two ingredients: arousal and concentration. This is exciting because it is easy to do. Once you become aware of what to tune into, the mind and body merge together in an experience Csiksentmihalyi calls **flow**. Here are some important characteristics of flow:

- Loss of ego is felt.
- Feeling of control predominates.
- Actions seem automatic, as in driving a car.
- There is little or no concern about winning, losing, or performing up to others' expectations; instead, gratification comes from the execution of the skill itself.
- Powers of anticipation and concentration become heightened.
- You feel confident without feeling cocky.

Consistency of the flow experience comes from disciplining yourself to stay within your own optimal level of arousal and finding interest in the details in which your concentration is absorbed.

18
Mental Techniques

Cognitive Strategy One

Ten-minute relaxation procedure: "Making the Mind Still as Water"

1. Sit in a comfortable chair.
2. Close your eyes.
3. Notice any tension in your muscles; if there is any tension, simply let the muscles relax.
4. Reinforce muscular relaxation by progressively going through each body area (i.e., legs, arms, shoulders, etc.) and letting relaxation occur.
5. Now let your mind be like water: empty, quiet, tranquil, and still.
6. If thoughts enter your mind, simply say "stop" to yourself.
7. If thoughts continue to busy your mind, focus on your breathing pattern.
8. Just "watch" your breath: notice as you inhale and exhale.
9. Focus on your breath until your mind is again still, quiet, and tranquil.
10. When ten minutes are up, slowly open your eyes.

Cognitive Strategy Two

How to prepare for a stressful situation subconsciously: "Promoting Harmony of the Mind"

1. Become aware of a potentially stressful situation; imagine it.
2. Instead of worrying, let your mind prepare you for the situation.
3. Whenever your mind feels as if it is about to be overcome by worry as you imagine the stressful situation, you can change this worry into a positive mental image. What is needed is a positive, alert, well-focused mind.
4. When you become aware of your worry, visualize the aspect of the situation that most causes the worry.
5. Focus on this worrisome aspect.

6. Ask yourself why this particular aspect causes you to worry.
7. If the answer to the question is based on something that you can change to alleviate the worry, visualize yourself making that change.
8. However, if your worry is based on something that you have no physical control over, go ahead and imagine the situation that causes worry.
9. Experience this worry with as many senses as possible (feel muscles tense, breathing quicken).
10. Interject a scene that is relaxing to you when the worry becomes intense.
11. Then go back to the stressful situation.
12. Each time the situation causes too much worry, spontaneously replace it with the relaxing scene.
13. Soon you will experience relaxation during the formerly stressful situation.

Cognitive Strategy Three

Benson's twenty-minute relaxation technique: "Relaxed Concentration"

Sit in a comfortable chair, close your eyes, and let the sound "one" be repeated over and over again within your mind. If any distractions occur, let them pass through, and then return to "one." Let this sound go through your mind at any rhythm for about twenty minutes.

Suggestions: Do not practice the relaxation technique after eating. Do not stop yourself with an alarm; instead, when you feel that twenty minutes are up, open one eye, glance at a clock, and come out of it naturally and easily, taking about thirty seconds to open your eyes.

Comments: Too much tension in the body causes a waste of energy. Also, there is simultaneous contraction of muscles in the body that can cause coordination problems. This contraction occurs because the muscles are so "wired up" that they cannot contract and relax at opportune moments. When there is too much anxiety, the thinking process also is distorted, sometimes causing a change in strategy or improper decision making because of a tense atmosphere. Finally, the focus of your attention may be directed inward and not on the proper cues. For example, in a study performed on beginning and advanced parachutists, it was found that advanced jumpers were less nervous than beginners just before the jump. The reason appeared to be that the advanced individuals were thinking about the strategy of the jump, while the beginners were focusing their thoughts inward on their feelings of anxiety.

The relaxation technique has been found to bring an individual into what might be described as a fourth state of consciousness (the other three states being wakefulness, deep dreamless sleep, and dreaming). This fourth state of consciousness has been found to be beneficial in relieving the body of stress. As oxygen consumption, heart rate, lactic acid, and general metabolic processes are decreased, the individual enters a more subtle level of consciousness. On this plane thoughts do not exist, and even the "one" sound may disappear, leaving no thought.

Never be concerned when you are practicing the relaxation technique. Even if a "no-thought mind" occurs, it is perfectly natural. The key is to let the "one" happen and just flow with the experience.

Although your first few attempts at the relaxation technique may take anywhere from ten to twenty minutes, regular practice can shorten the process to less than three minutes. The ability to trigger total relaxation in less than three minutes will serve you well in all your endeavors.

Cognitive Strategy Four

How to conquer fear: "Gaining Inner Strength"

1. Realize that if you do not tighten up physically when you become fearful, fear will not overcome you.
2. When you become afraid, monitor your muscles; notice if they become tense.
3. Also, notice if your breathing speeds up, your eyes dilate, or your teeth grit.
4. If these things do occur, use a "mini-relaxation technique" to decrease all this tension (see Cognitive Strategy Thirteen).

Another way to conquer fear:

1. Use your imagination to visualize the worst thing that could possibly happen during your feared experience.
2. Realize that if it is a self-defense situation, you may have another chance; if you miss a technique, you can try again.
3. If you fear injury, remember that focusing on the fear can only serve to increase your chances of injury because you are taking your concentration away from the task involved (i.e., if concerned about injury in a street situation, you may lose concentration and lose everything).
4. Therefore, remember that fear alone is the only thing that you should shy away from. Focus on the proper cues and there is no need for fear.
5. Immediately employ your relaxation procedure even though you are still experiencing the fearful event in your mind.
6. Now, although you are "in" the event that should be frightening, you do not feel any physiological symptoms of fear. Your relaxation technique conquered those symptoms, breaking fear's grip on your psyche.

Cognitive Strategy Five

How to use free time to improve performance: "Seize Each Moment"

1. Whether performing a monotonous activity (e.g., practicing stomach exercises) or just relaxing, you can let your mind wander to a proper focus of attention and improve your skills by using mental imagery.
2. Think about an imaginary self-defense situation: see it, feel it. See what the outcome will be.

3. If the outcome of your mental strategy fails, try another strategic approach.
4. Later, practice your imagined techniques physically.
5. Use trial and error. Be creative; make mental imagery fun!

Cognitive Strategy Six

How to conquer pain: "Promote Mind–Body–Spirit Unity"

(Be careful not to use this pain-control technique to mask or hide actual physical injury. This section is designed to help you deal with psychological pain and with the fatigue and pain of hard physical training.)

1. Realize first that pain exists only in your mind.
2. Know and have confidence that you can beat pain.
3. When you begin to feel the pain, go with it, use it, and realize that this pain is helping you to achieve a goal (e.g., the pain of high-intensity physical training).
4. Knowing that it is good, try to increase the pain.
5. The pain is being changed by you into a tool that helps you to know that you are reaching your limit.
6. You become objective about the pain, without emotional involvement.
7. The pain is something you merely attempt to heighten in order to achieve your goal. Without emotional involvement seek out pain; crave it.

Another way to conquer pain:

1. Realize that you have the power to control your thoughts.
2. Your mind can completely focus on only one thing at a time.
3. Therefore, when pain becomes excruciating, change your focus of attention to something else.
4. Focus on your favorite resting place, or the goal to which you aspire, or someone you love—in short, something that is pleasant to you.
5. Hold that focus of attention on something else and the pain will pass.

Cognitive Strategy Seven

How to monitor anxiety: "Body Awareness Control"

1. Monitor your present level of anxiety: Muscles tense or relaxed? Breathing fast or slow? Mental activity clear or cluttered?
2. Overall, is your arousal level too high, too low, or just right?
3. If it is too high, imagine that you are in a less stressful, less demanding situation. For example, if anxiety is too high prior to an intense sparring match, imagine that you will merely be shadow boxing or lightly sparring with a friend.

CHAPTER 18 MENTAL TECHNIQUES   77

4. If it is too low, imagine that the situation is far more demanding than it actually is. For instance, if you have trouble getting your excitement level high enough before a classroom session, imagine that your safety depends on the correct practice of your techniques.

Cognitive Strategy Eight

How to get excited about practice using imagery: "Revitalizing Chi"

1. Close your eyes; relax; let your body and mind become quiet and still.
2. Now imagine yourself in a self-defense classroom situation; see, hear, and totally experience the practice with as many senses as you can.
3. Feel your body going through the techniques. It is exciting because you feel that you are there.
4. Your senses, your muscles, and all parts of you are totally encompassed in the visualization that your mind has produced: feel it.
5. The scene in your mind changes so that you see yourself enjoying the satisfaction of an excellent performance (confidence, weight loss, energy, etc.).
6. Let this scene be with you until you realize you are excited about practicing.
7. Slowly open your eyes and prepare yourself for practice.

Cognitive Strategy Nine

Using music to get motivated: "Energize Chi"

1. Turn on your favorite tune (particularly music that is stimulating).
2. With eyes open or closed, imagine the situation in which you wish to become motivated.
3. Physically feel your muscles moving with the rhythm of the music as you become lost in the image of practicing your self-defense skills.
4. As in shadow boxing, let your muscles subtly move with the beat, performing optimally in your imagination.
5. Go out and perform.
6. If there is still a lack of motivation during practice or performance, turn on your favorite tune in your head, hear the beat—and go!

Cognitive Strategy Ten

How to revitalize yourself during your daily routine: "Spark the Light Within You"

1. Find a reasonably quiet place, sit comfortably, and close your eyes.
2. Let your muscles relax, and begin to "watch" your breath; your body and mind will become quiet and still.
3. Experience a favorite resting place (e.g., the beach, mountains).

4. See, hear, and feel all the sensations of this place. You may hear the waves crashing against the shore, feel the coolness of the breeze, etc.
5. After ten minutes, open your eyes, fully refreshed, alert, and ready to continue your day.

Cognitive Strategy Eleven

Relaxation–imagery for home practice: "Programming Your Mind"
(Read the following into a tape recorder and listen to it while relaxed.)

You are a good self-defense student. You train hard and have done well in self-defense thus far. You realize from previous learning that relaxation–imagery may aid your performance and ability. In fact, studies have found relaxation–imagery to be beneficial to performance. For example, some researchers attached electrodes to a person's muscles while he was relaxed and involved in mental imagery and found that the same muscle impulses that are transmitted during physical performance were also transmitted during an imaginary recreation of that performance. Therefore, it is similar to getting a practice effect in self-defense while you are just lying down, relaxed, and listening to the suggestions.

Now you will take control over your own actions as you go through an imaginary self-defense class. In each relaxation–imagery sequence, you may become very involved with all of your senses as you do each technique up to your potential.

Now imagine yourself entering the gym or classroom and feeling a strong desire to begin your training. See yourself, the class, and your instructor as you prepare to begin your practice. As you go through warm-up exercises, stretches, and basic strikes, you see the instructor in front of you and hear your own movements, the movements of your classmates, and the commands of the instructor counting you through the techniques. Feel the sweat of your body, the action of your muscles, and the movement of the air as your limbs lash out. As you conclude, you feel very good about what you have done, and you look forward to the next phase of the workout, which is situps.

As the instructor initiates situps with the command, "Interlock your legs," you begin to perform each situp to the count of the instructor, and you begin to feel slight pain in your abdomen as you sweat freely. Hear your own breathing and the movements you are successfully completing. See the rest of the class struggling just as you are in order to complete the exercises. You have learned to separate physical pain from emotional pain. Even though your stomach may be searing with pain, you are completing each exercise to the best of your ability with only positive thoughts in mind. In fact, the pain becomes a signal that you are doing the exercises correctly and to the best of your ability, and that is good. You know that this pain will serve to improve your physical abilities.

As you conclude stomach work, you prepare yourself for sparring.

As we begin sparring, you line up opposite your opponent and proceed with the ceremonial bow. This bow triggers a feeling of relaxed alertness as you attack and defend, maintaining concentration on the proper cues, reaching your optimal level of arousal. Whether you have just scored a point or have just been scored upon, your emotions do not enter your mind. You execute techniques with excellent precision. Each technique has the necessary power and speed in order to be effective. You maintain a light, bouncy, relaxed posture as you continue to find the proper distance to thwart your opponent. Your timing is perfect as you attack and defend, flowing with each of your opponent's moves with beautiful precision. See the completion of the activity, and feel a tremendous sense of accomplishment that you have performed up to your potential.

Now that you have completed sparring in your mind's eye, you know that this session has had a very powerful influence on your performance. You know that each time you spar you will get better and better. Also, you know that part of your mind cannot tell the difference between an actual event and an imagined event. Therefore, each time that you practice sparring during relaxation–imagery it will be as if you have just completed a perfect practice session.

In a few moments you are going to come out of your relaxed state. As you come out of this relaxed state, you may feel very good about yourself, and very good about what you have accomplished in this session, knowing that it may have a tremendous positive impact on your performance.

Cognitive Strategy Twelve

Self-defense in the street: "Prepare for the Unexpected . . . Now!"

1. Close your eyes; relax.
2. Imagine a specific situation involving a need for actual self-defense; visualize the actual setting.
3. See yourself in this situation as an assailant begins to approach you.
4. Know that you must and can remain calm, using one of the preceding cognitive strategies if necessary.
5. See yourself physically handling the situation with perfect precision, using your skills to the best of your potential.
6. Execute whatever techniques are necessary to handle the situation.
7. Feel very good about both your mental and physical handling of the situation, knowing that if you practice often enough in your mind, if a situation actually occurs you will be prepared.
8. Imagery can be more real to you than an actual experience, because through your imagination you may involve all of your senses.
9. With imagery you may create a situation and recreate it thousands of times so that if it occurs in reality you will be ready.

Cognitive Strategy Thirteen

How to relax one minute prior to a performance situation: "Mini-Relaxation Technique"

1. Close your eyes and relax (ten seconds).
2. Monitor your breathing; notice the relaxing effect on your body (twenty seconds).
3. See, feel, and experience yourself as you are about to enter the impending situation; develop a strategy for this situation (ten seconds).
4. Now actually mentally experience the situation visually and with other senses until you seem actually to be there (twenty seconds).
5. Now do it!

PART FOUR
Evaluation

Suggested Instructors' Evaluation Guide

Students may be evaluated with a combination of performance and written tests. The performance test consists of single-skill techniques (including grappling holds), combinations, and sparring. The students' performances may be rated on a five-point Likert scale by breaking down skills, combinations, and sparring into the component parts of form, intensity, power, flexibility, and effectiveness.

Five students are rated at one time on each of the performance areas. For example, if the students are being tested on the reverse punch, each of the five students performs ten punches consecutively. During the performance of these ten punches, the instructor observes and then grades each of the five individuals. Because each of the students performs ten punches, this gives the instructor enough time to scan the technique and come up with an average score.

Other performance variables include combinations, sparring, flexibility, and muscular endurance. Combinations consist of having the subject performing a variety of techniques in rapid succession. In sparring, each subject uses techniques in a competitive setting with the instructor for a one-minute time period.

Flexibility of the hamstring and groin muscles may be assessed using the Leighton Flexometer, and muscular endurance of the abdominal region is measured using the two-minute situp test.

Finally, written examinations are administered in order to determine whether the students have adequate knowledge of passive resistance, street awareness, and other aspects of self-defense. Sample examinations follow.

Sample Rating Guide

Skill

Front kick	Backfist
Front punch	Overhead block
Knife-hand strike	Palm-heel strike
Side kick	Roundhouse kick
Reverse punch	Back kick

Combinations

Front kick–punch
Knife-hand strike–side kick
Reverse punch–side kick–reverse punch

Muscular endurance

Situps
Roundhouse kicks on wall

Sparring

Each student will spar with the instructor for one minute and will be rated on the following criteria: breathing, speed, power, endurance, flexibility, coordination, relaxation, and execution.

Rating Scale

	SKILL					COMBINATIONS					SPARRING				
	FORM	INTENSITY	POWER	FLEXIBILITY	EFFECTIVENESS	FORM	INTENSITY	POWER	FLEXIBILITY	EFFECTIVENESS	FORM	INTENSITY	POWER	FLEXIBILITY	EFFECTIVENESS
Student #1															
Student #2															
Student #3															
Student #4															
Student #5															

Sample Test 1

Please answer the following questions True or False to the left of each question.

_____ 1. Kicking an assailant to the head is an effective technique in a street situation.
_____ 2. The power in our punches and kicks comes from the stomach area.
_____ 3. It is a good idea to face your opponent slightly sideways rather than head on.
_____ 4. Kicking is your most powerful weapon in a fighting situation.
_____ 5. You should give your opponent time to secure his hold before you attempt to escape.
_____ 6. You should never run away from an opponent; you must make him pay for assaulting you.
_____ 7. Against an assailant with a gun or knife, you should attack the weapon (e.g., kick it out of his hand), not the man.
_____ 8. You should let the attacker strike you first so that your endocrine system will release adrenaline, making your counterattack more powerful.
_____ 9. If you have maimed your opponent and find that you have the opportunity to either run away or kill him, you should run away.
_____10. When an assailant throws a punch or kick at you, for a split second there is an opening for you to counterattack.
_____11. It is a good idea to keep your hands in your pockets if you know that you are about to be attacked.
_____12. In a street situation, plan on throwing just one technique. One punch or kick should do the job.
_____13. Exhaling with each punch or kick may aid in creating more power in your technique.
_____14. Proper awareness is the most important defensive tool that you may have in a street situation.
_____15. One of the best target areas to strike on your opponent is the groin.
_____16. When you are calm, your body is relaxed and your techniques are fast.
_____17. Excellent body condition (being in shape) probably will not be helpful to you in a street situation.
_____18. The defensive side kick should be aimed at the stomach of your opponent in a street situation.
_____19. Generally, you should act timid and unsure of yourself when an assailant is about to attack you.
_____20. In a street defense situation it is best always to keep your hands in fists, never using a clawing action with the fingers.

Sample Test 2

1. In a street defense situation, name two vulnerable body areas that may be attacked.

2. Why is conditioning (i.e., flexibility, strength, endurance) important in the practice of self-defense?

3. What is the most important area of the body to develop, according to the instructor?

4. Against an assailant with a weapon, you should attack the weapon. True or False?

5. Name three reasons why it would be beneficial to practice a relaxation technique.

6. On a scale from 1 to 10, rate the attitude we try to cultivate in dealing with a street defense situation, with "calm" represented by 1 and "excited" represented by 10.

7. Name two reasons for using the "kiai."

8. What specific area of the body does the power come from in most of the techniques practiced, according to the instructor?

9. Why do we practice with regularity? Give two reasons.

10. Upon completion of this course, we have greater confidence in our self-defense capabilities. True or False?

Sample Test 3

1. Is kicking to the head a good idea in a street situation? Why or why not?

2. When you know you are about to be confronted in the street at close range, you should keep your hands in your pockets. True or False?

3. In a street situation, is a roundhouse kick more effective striking with the ball of the foot or with the instep?

4. When an attacker is attempting to secure you in a hold, you should let him tighten his grip so that he feels confident before unleashing your defense. True or False?

5. Why is physical conditioning important in a street situation? Give two reasons.

6. Explain why the overhead block in its strictest form may not be appropriate for a self-defense situation.

7. Name two target areas for the defensive side kick in a street situation.

8. Which blocking technique is most effective for stopping an attack to your groin area?

9. It is important to keep the muscles flexed and tensed in a self-defense situation so your opponent cannot hurt you. True or False? Why or why not?

10. "Do not try to stop force; it is easier to redirect it. Learn more ways to preserve rather than destroy, avoid rather than check, check rather than hurt, hurt rather than maim, main rather than kill, for all life is precious nor can any be replaced."
    Comment on the preceding.

Appendix: Student Handouts

Student Handouts: Individualized Self-Defense

Instructions

The following questionnaires deal with various aspects of self-defense performance and competition. Your honest and accurate responses will help the instructor to understand some of the important factors in optimal self-defense performance and perhaps pave the way for more beneficial services to people like yourself. Your responses will be kept confidential. Thank you for your cooperation.

Biographical/Experience Data

Do you have any previous experience in self-defense or the martial arts? Explain.

Do you have any previous experience in sports or other athletic endeavors? Explain.

Do you have any previous experience in the practice of mental preparation techniques such as meditation, biofeedback, imagery, relaxation techniques, psyching-up strategies, etc.? Explain.

Handout One: Performance

1. Do you feel confident that you are mentally and physically preparing yourself as well as possible for your self-defense performance?

2. How does your body usually feel when you perform well?

3. How does your body usually feel when you perform poorly?

4. Have you ever thought much about the role that your thoughts, emotions, and feelings play in your self-defense performance?

5. When you have self-defense performance problems what do you think is interfering with your ability to perform maximally?

6. Do you really have the physical self-defense skills down?

7. When you perform well in self-defense do you have an explanation of why? Describe your feelings and thoughts in these situations.

8. How do your feelings and thoughts when you perform well differ from when you perform poorly?

9. What were you thinking and feeling before, during, and after your peak performances?

10. How do your thoughts and feelings differ when you perform poorly?

11. Do you have any idea as to why you perform so well in certain self-defense situations?

12. What do you think are the differences between problem and peak self-defense performances?

Handout Two: Performance

Do you have trouble getting yourself up or energized for performance in class?

1   2   3   4   5   6   7   8   9   10   11
No trouble   Some trouble   A lot of trouble

Do you have trouble concentrating during performance?

1   2   3   4   5   6   7   8   9   10   11
No trouble   Some trouble   A lot of trouble

Do you think about performing poorly in class?

1   2   3   4   5   6   7   8   9   10   11
Never   Sometimes   Always

Do you concentrate more on your own performance or on the performance of others in your class?

1   2   3   4   5   6   7   8   9   10   11
My own   Both   Others

When you perform your techniques, is your concentration "in the moment" or in the future or past?

1   2   3   4   5   6   7   8   9   10   11
In the moment   Somewhat in the moment   In the future or the past

Do you worry about making mistakes in a performance?

1   2   3   4   5   6   7   8   9   10   11
Never   Sometimes   Always

Do you talk to yourself while performing?

1 2 3 4 5 6 7 8 9 10 11
Never   Sometimes   Always

When you make an error in your performance do you become anxious?

1 2 3 4 5 6 7 8 9 10 11
Never   Sometimes   Always

Do you worry about "choking" prior to your performance?

1 2 3 4 5 6 7 8 9 10 11
Never   Sometimes   Always

Handout Three: Sparring

How anxious are you before your bout?

1 2 3 4 5 6 7 8 9 10 11
Not anxious   Somewhat anxious   Extremely anxious

How confident are you before your bout, in general?

1 2 3 4 5 6 7 8 9 10 11
Not confident   Somewhat confident   Extremely confident

Are you psychologically in control of the bout, or is your opponent?

1 2 3 4 5 6 7 8 9 10 11
I have no control   I am somewhat in control   I am definitely in control

Is your fighting style aggressive, defensive, counterattacker, or somewhat in between?

1 2 3 4 5 6 7 8 9 10 11
Defensive   Counterattacker   Aggressive

How tough would you describe yourself to be?

1 2 3 4 5 6 7 8 9 10 11
Not at all   Somewhat   Extremely

How effective is your favorite fighting technique?

1 2 3 4 5 6 7 8 9 10 11
Not effective   Somewhat effective   Extremely effective

Do you enjoy sparring?

1 2 3 4 5 6 7 8 9 10 11
Not at all   Somewhat   Extremely

Handout Four: Mental Technique

When you practice your technique, describe your arousal (anxiety) level.

1 2 3 4 5 6 7 8 9 10 11
Calm   Somewhat anxious   Anxious

What do you do if your mind wanders while you are practicing your technique?

1	2	3	4	5	6	7	8	9	10	11
Try harder					Let it come				Give up	

How many times per week do you practice your technique?

1	2	3	4	5	6	7	8	9	10	11
Once a week					More than four days a week					Every day

Do you feel comfortable (familiar) with your technique?

1	2	3	4	5	6	7	8	9	10	11
Uncomfortable					Somewhat comfortable					Very comfortable

Did you understand the instructor's explanation and comments concerning your strategy?

1	2	3	4	5	6	7	8	9	10	11
Not at all					Somewhat				Very much so	

How many minutes per day do you practice your technique?

1	2	3	4	5	6	7	8	9	10	11
One minute or less					More than five minutes					Ten minutes

Do you feel that this technique is aiding your self-defense performance?

1	2	3	4	5	6	7	8	9	10	11
Not at all					Somewhat				Extremely	

Do you plan to continue to use some form of this technique after the semester is over?

1	2	3	4	5	6	7	8	9	10	11
Not at all					Sometimes				Definitely	

Were you able to incorporate these strategies into your lifestyle?

1	2	3	4	5	6	7	8	9	10	11
Not at all					Sometimes				Very much	

Handout Five: Cognitive Strategy

1. How useful do you feel that your cognitive strategy was in aiding your performance?

1	2	3	4	5	6	7	8	9	10	11
Not useful					Somewhat useful				Extremely useful	

2. Do you feel that your cognitive strategy would benefit performers in other sports?

1	2	3	4	5	6	7	8	9	10	11
Not at all					Somewhat				Very much	

3. Did you receive enough personal attention from the instructor in order to make the technique valuable to you?

1	2	3	4	5	6	7	8	9	10	11
Not at all					Somewhat				Definitely	

4. Do you feel that your cognitive strategy aided your performance?

1	2	3	4	5	6	7	8	9	10	11
Not at all					Somewhat				Very much	

5. Did you attempt to practice your cognitive strategy regularly?

   1 2 3 4 5 6 7 8 9 10 11
   Not at all   Somewhat   Very regularly

6. Did you understand the procedures for your cognitive strategy?

   1 2 3 4 5 6 7 8 9 10 11
   Not at all   Somewhat   Very much

7. Do you plan to ever use your cognitive strategy after the completion of the semester?

   1 2 3 4 5 6 7 8 9 10 11
   Not at all   Somewhat   Very much

8. Would you recommend this technique to others?

   1 2 3 4 5 6 7 8 9 10 11
   Not at all   Somewhat   Definitely

9. Did you gain any insight into yourself through the use and practice of your cognitive strategy?

   1 2 3 4 5 6 7 8 9 10 11
   Not at all   Somewhat   Very much

10. Would you be interested in learning and practicing another cognitive strategy designed to improve your performance?

    1 2 3 4 5 6 7 8 9 10 11
    Not at all   Somewhat   Very much

Handout Six: Street Awareness

1. How far must you walk from your vehicle to your place of employment?
   a. Are other people in the area?
   b. Is the area well lighted?

2. If someone followed you down the street, what would you do?

3. Is your home secure (locks on doors, screens or bars on windows, etc.)?

4. Do you have personalized license plates?

5. Do you check your back seat before you enter your vehicle?

6. Are you capable of using weapons such as keys, umbrella, etc.?

7. Have you thought out what you might do in a life-threatening self-defense street situation?

8. Have you mentally prepared yourself to use passive resistance strategies if the opportunity presents itself?

9. Are you prepared to inflict serious physical damage on an attacker?

10. Do you walk with confidence and relaxed alertness in the streets?

Bibliography

Bell, K. Relaxation training for competitive swimming. *Swimming Technique,* 1976, *13* (2), 14-43.
Benson, H. *The Relaxation Response.* New York: William Morrow & Co., 1975.
Desiderato, O. & Miller, I. B. Improving tennis performance by cognitive behavior modification techniques. *Behavior Therapist,* 1979, *2,* 19.
Epstein, M. L. The relationship of mental imagery and mental rehearsal to performance of a motor task. *Journal of Sport Psychology,* 1980, *2,* 211-220.
Feltz, D. & Landers, D. The effects of mental practice on motor skill learning and performance: A meta analysis. *Journal of Sport Psychology,* 1983, *5,* 25-27.
Gallway, T. *Inner Tennis: Playing the Game.* New York: Random House, 1976.
Herrigal, E. *Zen in the Art of Archery.* New York: Vintage Books, 1971.
Kirchenbaum, D. & Bale, R. Cognitive-behavioral skills in golf: Brain power golf. In R. Suinn (Ed.) *Psychology in Sports: Methods and Applications.* Minneapolis: Burgess, 1980, pp. 334-343.
Martens, R. Sports Competitive Anxiety Test II. Arousal and motor performance. *Exercise and Sport Science Reviews,* 1976, 20-38.
Meichenbaum, D. & Cameron, R. The clinical potential of modifying what clients say to themselves. *Psychotherapy: Theory, Research and Practice,* 1974, *11,* 103-117.
Meyers, A. & Schleser, R. A cognitive behavioral intervention for improving basketball performance. *Journal of Sport Psychology,* 1980, *2,* 69-73.
Meyers, A., Schleser, R., Cooke, C. & Cuvillier, C. Cognitive contributions to the development of gymnastics skills. *Cognitive Therapy & Research,* 1979, *3,* 75-85.
Richardson, A. Mental practice: A review and discussion: Part II. *Research Quarterly,* 1976, *38,* 263-273.
Ryan, E. & Simons, J. Cognitive demand, imagery, and frequency of mental rehearsal as factors influencing acquisition of motor skills. *Journal of Sport Psychology,* 1981, *3,* 35-45.
Schramm, V. *An Investigation of EMG Responses Obtained During Mental Practice.* Madison: University of Wisconsin Press, 1967.
Silva, J. Performance enhancement in competitive sports environments through cognitive intervention. *Behavior Modification,* 1981.
Sonstroem, R. & Bernardo, P. Intraindividual pregame state anxiety and basketball performance: A reexamination of the inverted-U curve. *Journal of Sport Psychology,* 1982, *4,* 235-245.
Spielberger, C. (Ed.) *Theory and Research: Anxiety and Behavior.* New York: Academic Press, 1966.
Suinn, R. Body thinking: Psychology of Olympic champs. *Psychology Today,* 1976, *10,* 38-43.
Suinn, R. M. Imagery and sports. In A. Sheikh (Ed.) *Imagery, Current Theory, Research and Application.* New York: John Wiley & Sons, Inc., 1981.

Suinn, R. & Andrews, F. Psychological strategies of professional competitors. Unpublished manuscript, Colorado State University, 1978.

Weinberg, R. The relationship between mental preparation strategies and motor performance: A review and critique. *Quest,* 1981, *33* (2), 195-213.

Weinberg, R., Seabourne, T. & Jackson, A. Effect of visuo-motor behavior rehearsal, relaxation, and imagery on karate performance. *Journal of Sport Psychology,* 1981, *2,* 340-349.

White, K. D., Ashton, R. & Lewis, S. Learning a complex skill: Effects of mental practice, physical practice, and imagery ability. *International Journal of Sport Psychology,* 1979, *10,* 71-78.